SEASONS OF MY MILITARY STUDENT

Practical Ideas for Parents and Teachers

An **Elva Resa** Book

By Amanda Trimillos
and Stacy Allsbrook-Huisman

Elva Resa ＊ Saint Paul

Seasons of My Military Student: Practical Ideas for Parents and Teachers
Text and art ©2018 Elva Resa Publishing.

Written by Amanda Trimillos and Stacy Allsbrook-Huisman for Elva Resa.
Edited by Terri Barnes for Elva Resa. Art by Brenda Harris for Elva Resa.
Seasons of Transition™ concept development by Karen Pavlicin-Fragnito.

Library of Congress Cataloging-in-Publication Data
Names: Trimillos, Amanda, author. | Allsbrook-Huisman, Stacy.
Title: Seasons of my military student : practical ideas for parents and teachers
  / Amanda Trimillos and Stacy Allsbrook-Huisman.
Description: St. Paul, MN : Elva Resa, [2018]
Identifiers: LCCN 2018002706 (print) | LCCN 2018011615 (ebook) |
  ISBN 9781934617441 (ePub) | ISBN 9781934617458 (Kindle) |
  ISBN 9781934617427 (pb)
Subjects: LCSH: Children of military personnel--Education--United States. |
  Education--Parent participation--United States.
Classification: LCC LC5081 (ebook) | LCC LC5081 .T75 2018 (print) |
  DDC 370.8--dc23
LC record available at https://lccn.loc.gov/2018002706

Printed in United States of America.
10 9 8 7 6 5 4 3 2 1

Published by Elva Resa Publishing
8362 Tamarack Vlg., Ste. 119-106, St. Paul, MN 55125

Elva Resa® is a registered trademark of Elva Resa Publishing.
™ Seasons of Transition™ property of Elva Resa Publishing.

ElvaResa.com
MilitaryFamilyBooks.com
Bulk discounts available.
Also available: *Seasons of My Military Student Action Guide*
SeasonsOfMyMilitaryStudent.com

To our own military-connected kids
and all military kids everywhere,
serving the United States of America
in their everyday lives.

To my four children.
I know you will grow and flourish
wherever the Lord brings you.
Thank you for your service to our nation as milkids.
Love, Mom

To my sturdy and beautiful dandelion kids:
Erik and Abby.
I can't wait to see where the winds will carry you next.
Love, Mom

CONTENTS

AUTHORS' NOTE

The dandelion is the unofficial flower of military children. It sends out its seeds to float on the wind, ready to settle in, put down roots, and grow anywhere. It produces bright sunny flowers, even in difficult circumstances.

While writing this book, we each guided our own dandelion children through various seasons of growth in their military lives.

We based our recommendations in this book on research, our own personal experiences as military parents, our professional expertise in education and communication, and interviews with other military families and colleagues.

As we have watched our own children travel to new locations, put down roots, grow and thrive, we are impressed over and over by the tenacity, dedication, and resilience of military-connected students. It is our hope that the concepts and guidelines in this book will inform and inspire parents and teachers to create greater educational continuity for many more indomitable dandelion kids.

INTRODUCTION

Continuity—educational, social, and emotional—is essential for the success and growth of all students, from pre-K through high school graduation. A student masters a set of skills at each level in order to move on to the next. For children in military families, cultivating continuity requires a strong team of adult advocates who understand the unique challenges of military life and their impact on a student's education.

Seasons of My Military Student: Practical Ideas for Parents and Teachers is a guidebook to help parents and teachers work together to support and advocate for military-connected students as they experience Seasons of Transition™ and the storms that may arise in any season of military life.

Military parents have long recognized the effects of military life on their children and their children's education. Research backs up that hard-won knowledge. Independent reports and studies reveal that growing resilient children amid the events of military life—frequent moves, family separations, combat loss and injury—requires intentional support strategies. The insights and tips shared in *Seasons of My Military Student* are based on findings from this research combined with professional experience and first-hand perspectives from military families and educators.

Military students may attend public, private, or home-based schools. One of these, or a combination of education choices, may fit the needs of mobile military families as they guide their children through their school years.

For any education option, the challenges are not purely academic. Military-connected students are concerned about making good friends as well as good grades, and healthy social adjustment plays a part in positive educational growth.

To facilitate an understanding of the cycle of transitions a military-connected student experiences, this book divides the key transition points into four Seasons of Transition: Leaving, Arriving, Growing, and Thriving. Like the four seasons of nature, the Seasons of Transition follow a natural lifecycle of planting, nurturing, growing, and harvesting. In each season, a student has the opportunity to gain coping skills and resiliency, while progressing through the academic and social journey of changing schools, enduring deployments, and addressing other challenges of military life.

In the Season of Leaving, a student prepares to say goodbye to familiar surroundings. In the Season of Arriving, a student is transplanted to a new location. In the Season of Growing, a student begins to sprout and put down roots, becoming integrated into the new school culture. In the Season of Thriving, a student blossoms, building self confidence, exploring passions, nurturing deeper friendships, and developing resilience for the next transition.

Heavy weather can happen during any season of military life. Deployments and other family separations are common examples of storms that have the potential to disrupt a student's learning. When severe storms, such as combat injury or loss, occur in military families, the effects are more far reaching and profound. The chapter Storms in Any Season is dedicated to strategies for supporting military-connected students in difficult situations.

Partnership and solid communication are the best shelter parents and educators can offer a military-connected student in any season or storm. The student-advocacy team begins with parents and classroom teachers, with close support from counselors and school administrators. This partnership also

---

Partnership and solid communication are the best shelter parents and educators can offer a military-connected student in any season or storm.

SEASONS OF TRANSITION

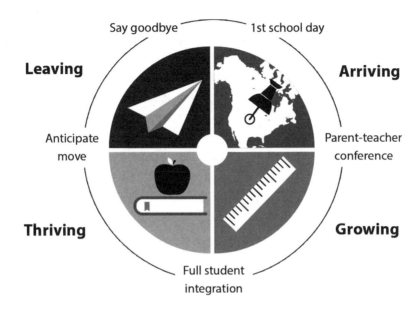

brings the student alongside, ultimately giving the maturing student confidence to self-advocate.

The right tools of cultivation are essential to the success of the student and the student-advocacy team. One of these tools is knowledge of the provisions of the Interstate Compact on Educational Opportunity for Military Children, which addresses key education issues faced by military-connected students related to enrollment, eligibility, placement, and graduation.

Another core tool is the Seasons Education Binder. This repository of important documentation and information becomes a portable record of a student's strengths and needs, traveling with the student to each new school. The companion resource *Seasons of My Military Student Action Guide* includes clear guidance for creating an Education Binder, as well as sample letters, activity records, and divider pages to create personalized support for the student in every season.

Creating a record of academic history is important, whether the student is changing schools or maintaining a detailed record of education completed at home or online. The binder provides a unified record and a way to communicate a student's educational progress beyond a transcript of grades.

Continuity can be cultivated even in transitions, and healthy growth happens in every season, from the Season of Leaving to the Season of Thriving. Seasons change and storms will come, but when properly nurtured and cultivated, the student's resilience and education will move forward with stability. Potential for growth is present in the seed, as well as in the flower.

THE TEAM & TOOLS OF
CULTIVATION

Cultivating healthy growth, for gardens and for students, requires people who care, awareness of the environment, and the right tools. Some tools are used to create conditions conducive to growth; other tools are used to prepare the student to flourish in various environments and seasons. Tools of cultivation for military-connected students include:

- 🖊 An understanding of the challenges of military life and the Seasons of Transition

- 🖊 Knowledge of the provisions of the Interstate Compact on Educational Opportunity for Military Children

- 🖊 A consistent record of a student's progress

These tools, when used by a strong student-advocacy team, provide continuity for the growing, thriving student, both personally and academically.

IDENTIFY THE STUDENT

A military-connected child is any child who has a parent or guardian serving in the armed forces. This includes all branches of the military, both active duty and reserve components, as well as National Guard units. Schools located near military installations, and those operated by the Department of Defense Education Activity (DoDEA) naturally serve students who are connected to the military, but they are not the only schools serving military-connected students.

In fact, military-connected students may be present in any school district in the United States. Families connected to National Guard or reserve units, as well as those on recruitment assignments, may live far from a military installation. Students who attend a school without the support of a nearby military community may need even more support and understanding from their educators.

Meeting the needs of military-connected students begins with identifying them. A 2010 study, "School Transitions Among Military Adolescents," published in *School Psychology Review*, reported that educators are often unable to identify military-connected students in their schools.

The Every Student Succeeds Act of 2015 (ESSA) includes a provision that now requires federally-funded schools to identify military-connected students and track performance factors such as test scores and graduation rates. ESSA also requires each US state to publish an annual report card.

Federal Impact Aid surveys identify federally-connected students—including those from military families—for school funding purposes. Participation in this voluntary annual survey offers military families an opportunity to self-identify and connect with public schools. Teachers who are aware of military-connected students in the classroom can encourage the student or parent to complete the forms. Military parents can add emphasis to the survey by attaching a note to the form or by returning the form to the school office in person, opening another avenue of communication with the school.

The Department of Education uses Federal Impact Aid to supplement school districts that have lost a portion of local tax base because of federally-owned land and to help school districts that educate a set minimum attendance rate of federally-connected students. More funding and more information helps schools, educators, and students.

BUILD THE TEAM

A strong student-advocacy team begins with those who are most invested in the student. Parents are the student's primary supporters as she moves from school to school and teacher to teacher. Teaming up with teachers and other educators is the best action parents can take to provide opportunities for educational success. An attentive teacher can also initiate the team on behalf of the student, encouraging parents to embrace the concept and take the lead for the next transition.

The team, whether initiated by parent or teacher, grows stronger when each member respects the skills and knowledge of the other. While the parents are key to ensuring continuity, they are wise to seek teachers' classroom perspective. Likewise, teachers should respect parents' knowledge of their child. The relationship is built on trust, respect, and strong communication. Both parents and teachers, as well as connecting with one another, should keep lines of communication open with the student, involving him in decisions and discussions as appropriate at each grade level.

Parents and children experience the transitions of military life from different perspectives. Teachers and transitioning students view the classroom differently from their respective desks in the classroom. When parents and teachers recognize the challenges of military life from a student's viewpoint, they can become even better advocates.

RECOGNIZE THE CHALLENGES

Military life puts many students in a recurrent state of transition, adjustment, and adaptation. Frequent moves and changes of environment—new homes, schools, and neighborhoods—require establishing new peer groups and routines, learning cultural nuances, and adapting to different climates. Lengthy time apart from a deployed parent means learning how to communicate effectively over distance, and adjusting and readjusting to changes in rules and

> When parents and teachers recognize the challenges of military life from a student's viewpoint, they can become even better advocates.

routines at home as parents separate and reintegrate. Some students are exposed to injury or death of service members in their community or their own families. Collectively, these experiences mold a student's perspective and test her capacity to positively cope and develop valuable life skills.

The resilience required to thrive in military life is not the automatic result of being born into a military family. Resilience grows when military-connected students are nurtured by support networks at home, at school, and in the community.

The Future of Children, a journal published by Princeton University and the Brookings Institution, produced an issue in 2013 titled "Military Children and Families," in cooperation with the Military Child Education Coalition (MCEC). The article "Resilience Among Military Youth" reported that the stressors of military life can positively impact a military child if the child is adequately supported during times of stress. The study also found that military children with strong connections to parents, peers, and the community adjust better to the challenges of frequent moves, deployment, and injury.

A study published in *Military Medicine*, the journal of the Society of Federal Health Professionals (formerly Association of Military Surgeons of the United States), found that military-connected children who move more frequently may experience greater difficulty making new friends, may struggle more in school, and could have more emotional and behavioral issues.

However, the study also found that the largest contributing factor among well-adjusted military children was a positive relationship with their parents. Good family relationships provide a buffer for the stress a military family endures.

Active duty families move about every two to three years. Military families connected to National Guard or reserve components usually move less often, but still experience the effects of deployment, sometimes without a supportive military community nearby. In fact, almost all military families, whether active duty, guard or reserve, experience deployment.

The resilience required to thrive in military life is not the automatic result of being born into a military family. Resilience grows when military-connected students are nurtured by support networks at home, at school, and in the community.

MCEC, in response to a request from the US Army, conducted a study about the impact of school policies, processes, and programs on the education of military-connected children. The resulting report, "Education of the Military Child in the 21st Century," published in 2012, affirms that academic challenges of military-connected students are often related directly to frequent moves. Widely-varying educational standards, curricula, and expectations from one school district to another create constantly changing landscapes for students when they move.

In interviews with students, parents, teachers, and school leaders, the MCEC study also found that the challenges military-connected families bring to a school have an impact on the way schools and classrooms operate. Likewise, support from the school directly affects a student's capability to adapt and achieve. For example, parents who received a high level of support from a school reported a positive or neutral impact of deployment on a child's education. Parents who received unhelpful or ambivalent responses from a school reported negative educational impact during deployment.

Though focused on students in army families, the study's results reflect and validate the anecdotal evidence of military parents and their children in all service branches.

A 2014 study titled "Military Parents' Perceptions of Public School Supports for Their Children" similarly concluded that public school support for military-connected students can magnify the positive impact of a supportive family and military community.

The resilient qualities of military-connected students are cultivated and reinforced by strong support systems at home, at school, and in the community.

FAST FACT

The **Department of Defense Education Activity** operates preschool through high school education programs for military-connected students at installations throughout the US and overseas.

According to DoDEA, a military-connected student moves six to nine times during a school career, an average of three times more often than students from civilian families.

DoDEA.edu

Parents, knowing their experiences are backed up by research, can better communicate needs and challenges to educators and schools. For teachers, these studies and reports provide valuable information for developing tools and strategies to help military-connected students succeed.

KNOW THE INTERSTATE COMPACT

Educational rules and regulations vary from state to state and school to school regarding kindergarten enrollment age, acceptance to special education programs, placement in honors classes, high school graduation requirements, class ranking, and more. These variations can create educational challenges for students in mobile military families.

To addresses these challenges, an advisory group convened by the Council of State Governments and the Department of Defense crafted the Interstate Compact on Educational Opportunity for Military Children. The compact is applicable to interstate transfers between public schools in all fifty states, the District of Columbia, and DoDEA schools worldwide. It does not apply to transfers between private or home schools.

The compact supports military-connected students in kindergarten through high school, including children of US active duty military members, National Guard and reserve members who are on active duty orders, and other select US uniformed services. The compact also applies to children of military members who have died while on active duty for one year after the death of the military member, and, for up to one year, the children of medically-discharged or retired veterans.

The compact's governing body, Military Interstate Children's Compact Commission (MIC3), requires each state to designate a state commissioner to oversee implementation of the compact and to assist schools and parents with compact-related transitions. Compliance with the compact is part of each member state's statutes.

While the compact defers to state and local authority regarding curriculum, its provisions address other key areas of education that may help military-connected students avoid academic delays or penalties related to military life experiences.

Provisions of the Interstate Compact include:

- **Enrollment:** A student shall be allowed to continue enrollment at grade level, including attending kindergarten in the receiving state if previously enrolled in an accredited kindergarten in the sending state, even if the child does not meet the age requirement of the receiving state or school district.

- **Placement**: A student shall be placed in appropriate grade level subjects and classes at a new school and not be required to repeat similar classes due to varying state requirements. A student may continue in honors or advanced placement courses if the student had similar coursework in the sending state.

- **Special services**: A student may continue special education classes or gifted services in each state without waiting months to be evaluated. The receiving school may perform subsequent evaluations to ensure the student's placement and services are appropriate.

- **Exams**: The receiving state shall accept exit or end-of-course exams required for graduation from the sending state, national achievement tests, or alternative testing so the student can graduate on time.

- **Graduation**: A student shall be allowed to graduate on time if all academics are completed to meet graduation requirements of either the receiving or sending state.

READY RESOURCE

A downloadable version of the Interstate Compact on Educational Opportunity for Military Children, guidance about how to use it, and how to contact MIC3 state commissioners, are available at **MIC3.net**.

- ✎ **Extracurriculars**: The receiving school shall try to facilitate the student's participation in extracurricular activities, such as sports and school clubs, even if the student has missed tryout or enrollment dates.

- ✎ **Deployment-related absences**: A student shall be granted excused absences to spend extra time with a military parent who has been called to duty for, is on leave from, or has immediately returned from a combat-related deployment.

- ✎ **Student records**: Parents may receive copies of their student's educational records from the sending school to hand carry to a receiving school.

The Interstate Compact is not intended to give special treatment to military-connected students but to give them the same opportunities as their civilian peers, says Cherise Imai, executive director of the Military Interstate Children's Compact Commission.

"The compact covers the most common transition challenges that have the greatest impact on a student. It's important for parents to know what is covered and what is not," Imai says. "Military kids are just like every other kid. They want to succeed in school, and the compact is there to support them."

Toward the end of Sally's sophomore year in high school, her military dad received orders requiring the family to move a month before the end of the school year. Sally talked to all her teachers, knowing she would need to complete her end-of-year assignments and exams early to get full credit for her courses. The state where Sally lived required state-standardized testing for high school credits, and Sally's family was scheduled to leave before the state-mandated testing window. Sally's parents requested a waiver to allow her to take the tests early. The principal informed them the school did not have the authority to alter the state test dates. Without the tests, Sally could not receive credit for her tenth-grade classes. Sally's father could not change the date of his orders, so the family decided he would go ahead while the rest of the family remained behind for Sally's finals.

Sally's mom decided to make one last call—to the district superintendent. The superintendent had just returned from Interstate Compact training and gave Sally the waiver to take her tests early.

The Interstate Compact accommodates or influences solutions for many conflicts that arise for military-connected students who change schools. School personnel may not always be aware of its provisions. Parents can use their knowledge of the compact to empower the student-advocacy team.

A local school liaison officer (SLO) can also provide information about the compact and help with compliance. SLOs are assigned by their respective military service branch and support military-connected students in a variety of ways. They are charged with identifying barriers to academic success and helping families overcome those challenges. They also aid communication between a military command, military families, and schools. Parents can call on a SLO for any education issue, including school requirements, information about prospective schools during transitions, and support related to the compact.

MIC3 commissioners appointed by each state to administer the Interstate Compact are also available to help. MIC3 commissioners advise boards of education and have the authority to require local school districts to honor and adhere to the compact.

KEEP GOOD RECORDS

A portable Education Binder is a record of a student's progress, holding unofficial copies of grades and transcripts, as well as personal notes about social and emotional development, to give a fuller picture of a student's ability, personality, and progress. The Education Binder is a tool the student-advocacy team creates and uses together. It provides crucial documents and information about transitioning students, giving a new school and a new teacher a cohesive history of the student, and reducing the educational impact of changing schools.

> *Stacy has moved seven times—enough to know that orders can come unexpectedly, and moves can happen quickly. For these reasons, she doesn't wait until it's time to move to build Education Binders for both her children. Throughout each school year, she files away information about their progress in school. She keeps all standardized testing results, as well as work samples like spelling tests and writing assignments. She takes notes at every parent-teacher conference and prints out teacher emails that relate to her children's strengths, weaknesses, and progress throughout a school year. These become part of two Education Binders, one for her daughter and one for her son. Stacy keeps the binders with other important papers, ready for the next move to a new school.*

Military families hand-carry a variety of important documents during a permanent change of station (PCS). Among these should be an Education Binder for each student in the family.

The information in the Education Binder supplements official transcripts provided by one school for the next. The binder also serves as a backup if paperwork is late in arriving or lost in transit. Information from the binder can be shared with a new school counselor or administrator at registration, assisting in placement of a child in appropriate classroom settings. Information from the binder can also be shared with a new teacher, providing information about past issues and successes. Often placement in classes or in special services is made based on previous teacher recommendations in the spring for the following year. This can become a gap for military-connected students. The binder is one way to bridge that gap.

To be effective over multiple moves, the binder is best maintained by the parents. However, both parents and teachers can initiate these records.

In her DoDEA classroom, Ms. Massey helped her ninth and tenth grade math students maintain records to track their own progress in her class.

"Students were responsible for keeping a collection of their work in their own personal folders. I also asked them to keep a notebook," Ms. Massey says. "The main component of the notebook was a document that my co-teacher and I created that showed what standard was mastered, the section it aligned to, and how the student did. The student would color in blocks to show individual progress, and the other teacher and I would write notes on it as well. These sheets were stapled into their folders for easy access and could be referenced at any time to show student growth."

Ms. Massey asked her students to show their folders and notebooks and talk about their progress in meetings with parents. "The students did all the talking, and parents loved being able to see the work in the student's writing."

When it was time for students to move, the record they created went with them to give to a new math teacher. "There was plenty for them to share instead of just

FAST FACT

The **Family Educational Rights and Privacy Act** (FERPA) includes these rights for parents and guardians regarding their child's school records:

› Right to review or access a child's academic files maintained by the school

› Right to request that the school amend their child's files

› Right to file a FERPA violation complaint

Access to a student's files is crucial for military families, especially in transition. Schools are required by law to give parents copies of all academic records on file for their child.

www2.ED.gov/FPCO

a grade," Ms. Massey says. " I would write a short narrative (about the student) and add that into the folder."

Building an Education Binder can begin with material like the notebooks created by Ms. Massey's high school students, or it can begin with the first progress reports for a kindergartner. The sooner the better. The more information, the stronger the connection from one school to the next.

Vital information for a student's Education Binder includes:

- 🖊 **Shot records**: Shot records are needed to register for any new school. Often they are kept electronically, but consider keeping extra hard copies on hand. These are handy for applications for camps, sports, and child care providers, and any time an electronic copy is not available.

- 🖊 **Report cards**: Notes about substantial drops in grades may also be helpful, particularly if they occurred due to deployments, homecomings, mid-year moves, or health challenges.

- 🖊 **Schoolwork samples**: Include some homework assignments and tests from all classes and subjects, handwriting samples, personal essays, and other creative work. Input like this can influence honors class placement, remedial tutoring needs, and college preparation. Include work that shows the student's best abilities, as well as those that show weaknesses and a progression of improvement, to give the new teacher a holistic picture of the student.

- 🖊 **List of textbooks or workbooks used in class**: A list of texts, including book title, edition, and ISBN, will help receiving teachers know what materials the student has used and studied. Include completed workbooks to show the student's work when possible. This is especially important in mid-year moves when a student must complete a full grade level across different schools.

- **Reading list**: A list of the books a student has read, whether in class or independently, shows reading ability, range, and interests.

- **Standardized assessment results**: Testing varies from state to state, but test results are transferable, according to the Interstate Compact. Maintain a personal record of all standardized school testing, including state boards for special diplomas. Parents may request official copies of test results, rather than simply writing down scores, so the results can be verified.

- **High school graduation requirements**: The Interstate Compact provisions allow a transferring high school student to graduate on time if the requirements for graduation are met for the sending or receiving school. A copy of the standards from one school will be helpful at the next if a student's graduation date is in question.

- **Other evaluations**: Speech, occupational, and any other therapy reports, evaluations, and assessments, from the school or outside school agencies, help maintain continuity of services. The goal is to avoid losing the progress made in any therapy.

- **Conference notes**: Save any notes taken during conferences with teachers and school counselors throughout the year. These may help new schools align the student to a new teacher in the new location. These also help a new teacher see trends and strategies that were supported throughout the student's education.

- **Exceptional Family Member Program (EFMP) status**: Parents may choose to have documentation available in case it is needed to substantiate a student's need for an education plan. EFMP records are part of a military-connected student's medical history and do not have to be shared with the school.

 Individualized Education Plan (IEP), 504 Plan: Add a copy of the student's IEP or 504 Plan into the binder in case it is not forwarded in time for registration.

If a student has specific physical or educational needs and does not have a specialized education plan, parents or educators may request an evaluation at any time to determine if a plan is necessary. Parents also have the right to disagree with or to request an amendment to an existing plan, and to request mediation. All schools receiving federal funding are required by law to provide and act on these programs.

An Individualized Educational Plan is developed to ensure that a child with a disability receives specialized instruction and related services.

A 504 Plan is designed to ensure a child who has a disability receives accommodations that promote

READY RESOURCE

Enrollment in the **Exceptional Family Member Program** is for military family members of any age with special needs. These include:

› Conditions requiring special medical services

› Significant behavioral health concerns

› Situations or conditions calling for an Individualized Education Plan or 504 plan

This program covers a range of conditions with varying severity, for example: allergies, asthma, depression, attention deficit hyperactivity disorder (ADHD), diabetes, autism, or multiple sclerosis. The EFMP is intended to make sure military families can access information and support services they need.

EFMP status of military family members is taken into consideration when the service member is being assigned to a new duty location.

academic success, giving the student full access to the learning environment.

- **Awards**: Include a list of any classroom or school achievements and awards, with copies of certificates or a note from the school if possible. Include awards for winning or placing in a spelling or geography bee, math competition, athletic events, a role in the school play, essay competitions. These examples paint a more vibrant picture of the student for new school staff.

- **Copies of current school and sports physicals**: Annual physicals are often necessary for school enrollment and sports participation.

- **Teacher-to-teacher communication**: Include input from as many classroom teachers as possible, as well as music directors, club advisors, and coaches, if applicable. Broader input will present the student's range of aptitude in academic subjects as well as extracurriculars. If a student takes private lessons or coaching in any pursuit, a note from those private instructors could be helpful too.

- **Copy of the Interstate Compact**: It's a good idea to keep a copy of the compact on hand as a reference.

Good organization is essential. As the binder grows, divide the material into sections and create a table of contents to make the binder easy to navigate and share. *Seasons of My Military Student Action Guide* contains ready-made dividers and checklists for a convenient framework.

When sharing the binder with a new school, teacher, or counselor, determine what information is needed and share only what is pertinent to the situation. For example, a teacher doesn't need a student's shot records to determine the class seating arrangement, nor does an English teacher require letters from previous math or music teachers. Offering copies of specific and relevant input and student work samples optimizes the power of the binder.

Consider using a separate binder with copies of information a teacher or counselor needs time to review. Alternatively, parents may choose to remove sections from the binder to share or make copies of the necessary information. If a section of the binder is left with an educator, the parent should make a note in the table of contents as a reminder of where the material was left, with whom, and when it should be returned or picked up.

The Education Binder is a living document, growing and changing along with the student and tailored to his or her needs. With each transition, parents and teachers will add new material and may choose to remove material that is no longer relevant.

SEASON OF
LEAVING

The Season of Leaving begins with the anticipation and preparation for a move, which includes creating an exit plan. This season is usually the shortest and busiest one, because there is much to do for parents, teachers, and students: medical appointments, academic evaluations, documentation for the Education Binder, researching new schools, and farewell celebrations. All this activity is focused on preparing the student academically, socially, and emotionally for departure.

ANTICIPATION

Military families can feel it in the air when the season for a move draws near. Often orders come in spring, so perhaps the calendar initiates the anticipation. Or perhaps other families and close military friends already know they are moving.

Even very young military children begin to recognize the cycle of their lives, sometimes anticipating a move even before one is due. They may ask: "When will we move again?" or "How many more birthdays will I celebrate in this house?"

When stationed overseas, a family usually begins the assignment knowing the endpoint, the date of expected return from overseas (DEROS). Other assignments are less defined, and for parents, the difficulty in answering their children's questions is that they echo their own.

A military family is usually aware of the next move, though the timing may be uncertain. That uncertainty—when the family is anticipating news about a move, or when friends are moving—can create stress for a child.

When Jason's first-grade teacher asked her students to raise their hands if they would return to the same school the next year, Jason kept his hand at his side. His best friend's family was moving, so Jason thought his family might move too. The teacher followed up with a call to Jason's parents and learned his family was not moving.

Jason's experience as a military child and his connection with his friend caused him to anticipate a move when one was not coming. Moving season in a military community can be confusing, especially for young children. For teachers of younger students, initial questions about moving are probably better addressed to parents. When a child's friend is preparing to move, military parents should talk with their child as well as their child's teacher. Whether military or civilian, a student whose friends are moving may need reassurance.

Anticipation of this season can be both positive and negative. Military families dream of all the locations around the world their military life could take them. At the same time, they are aware of impending goodbyes, as they anticipate leaving friends, school, neighborhood, and the comfortable routines established in their current home.

Some military families prefer to keep discussion about moving low-key until orders are definite, while others prefer to keep their children informed of any developments.

Parents and teachers know adventure awaits military-connected students, including new friends, a new school,

CONVERSATION

Teacher to parent

› When do you anticipate moving?

› What will we need to do if the move comes before the end of the school year?

› What type of emotional changes from the student do you anticipate?

› What friends will be the hardest for the student to leave?

and a new home. For adults, years of experience provide the advantage of perspective. A kindergartner, seventh grader, or high school junior may have a harder time taking in the big picture. Thoughts of leaving familiar faces and places loom large over the horizon.

Good parent-teacher communication is essential all year long, and those positive channels will be put to good use when a transition is coming. As soon as the likelihood of a move is established, and until the student moves or the school year ends, a new level of communication and cooperation between family and school is key.

Students will have questions that require honest, age-appropriate answers. Parents and teachers should listen carefully to questions and what they convey about a student's feelings. Teachers will need to know how parents are responding to the student's questions and vice-versa, so the student-advocacy team stays on the same page.

> *Katy wanted to play an instrument in the school band, but she knew her military family had orders to move. When the instrument applications were distributed at school, she threw hers away without even bothering to bring it home or tell her mom about her desire to play. Katy didn't think her wishes mattered because she was changing schools. She thought she wouldn't be able to sign up for band at either school.*

When a transition is approaching, it's important to talk about all facets of the coming school year. Parents can ask their children what programs they might want to join at their next school. More conversation about the possibilities would have alerted Katy's mom and teacher about Katy's desire to join band, and Katy could have registered for an instrument. Acceptance into a program in a current school may transfer to acceptance into a similar program in a new school. Also, orders sometimes get canceled—another point of uncertainty for military families—and Katy's application would qualify her to join the band in her current school.

Near the end of Erik's fifth grade year, he knew his family would be moving over the summer. When his school offered a tour of the middle school he would attend if he were staying, he was uncertain whether he should attend. His mom encouraged him to take the tour so he could get an idea of what to expect in sixth grade. He could also experience with his classmates the excitement of getting ready for middle school.

Jason's, Katy's, and Erik's stories show how an approaching season of transition can create anxiety for students, and how good communication can alleviate some of the stress.

Rarely does a student like to say goodbye to teachers, friends, and familiarity, even when eager for a new adventure. Anticipation of a move brings a range of emotions for the student who is moving as well as the student's friends.

Weeks before Abby's family was scheduled to move, friends on the playground stopped inviting her to play. Abby felt left out. After a series of unhappy experiences, Abby's mom spoke to the teacher and to the parents of some of Abby's friends to make them aware of the situation. Mom chatted with the playground monitors, asking them to watch for signs of isolation. The most important call she made was to the school counselor.

The counselor created a girls' lunch in the classroom and talked to the students about change, what it looks like and feels like to different people. The girls talked through their conflict calmly with guidance from the counselor. Soon, Abby's smile returned. Friends were including her again. She had a new understanding of how her friends were feeling about her move. It is natural for kids to withdraw from a friend who is leaving and to migrate toward those who are staying, but Abby's friends didn't intend to hurt her. Having an adult point out opportunities for empathy and understanding helped repair hurt feelings before it was time for Abby to say goodbye.

Experience teaches military families like Abby's that some of their friends will begin to withdraw when a move is announced. Birthday invitations stop coming, play dates and get-togethers become fewer. Parents may expect this and even understand it to some degree, but the child doesn't. When friends and classmates pull away, the emotional impact of this season is compounded.

For this reason, sometimes a family may choose to keep news of a coming move quiet until the event is imminent. At the same time, it may be necessary or advisable to let a teacher or counselor know about the move. Bringing a teacher into the confidential communication will strengthen the team. It is essential, then, that teachers respect a family's wishes about the timing of announcing a move to the class or other friends.

PREPARATION

When parents are ready to share the news of a move with teachers, the team can prepare for departure by creating an exit plan. The exit plan includes a timeline that takes into account all the events, tasks, and actions that lead up to the student's last day of class, such as due dates for classroom projects and exams, opportunities for farewell parties, and school withdrawal procedures.

A well-executed exit plan means a smooth transition—academically, socially, and emotionally—building a student's confidence and ability to cope with future transitions.

PARENT POINTER

Once a relocation is confirmed, positive conversations about a fresh start and potential new experiences can help a student build excitement.

Encourage the student to brainstorm and research:

› Interesting facts about and places to explore in the new location

› Possible travel routes to get there

› Common fun phrases or customs practiced in the new location

› New activities to try at a new school, such as a different sport, an art class, or trying out for a school play

Every move is different, and the timeline is customized accordingly, depending on factors such as the geographic distance of the move and the amount of time between notification and departure. The military may notify a family of a move weeks or months before issuing official military orders, the paperwork that authorizes a move. The military member must have this paperwork to set the events of a move in motion, from scheduling the pickup of household goods to choosing a new home.

Still, some tasks on the timeline, such as scheduling medical appointments, can be accomplished ahead of time, even before receiving official orders. Others are date-specific and will be determined when the orders are in hand, such as the dates for packers and movers, or the student's last day of class.

Here are a few steps the team can take to prepare for a forthcoming move:

BEGIN STUDENT PAPERWORK

- Check school withdrawal procedures. Find out the procedure and timelines for withdrawal from the current school, ensuring that necessary records are prepared and ready.

- Update medical records. Be sure immunizations are current. Schedule appointments for student physicals, if the receiving school will accept a valid physical from another location. This may save the stress of getting in to see a new physician immediately after a move.

- Initiate or update specialized education plans. Most schools have a mechanism for parents to request an evaluation for a student's need for special services, such as occupational or speech therapy, English as second language, reading assistance, gifted and talented identification, or an IEP or 504 plan.

A well-executed exit plan means a smooth transition—academically, socially, and emotionally—building a student's confidence and ability to cope with future transitions.

If a new evaluation is needed, it should be requested as soon as possible. Testing and evaluations for services can take up to several weeks or months to complete. If a parent believes a child needs educational services, this is a good time to start the referral process. Parents may discuss options and qualifications with the child's current teacher as well as other professionals in the school. It makes sense to initiate this process with educators who are familiar with a child, personally and academically.

If the student already has an education plan, this is the time to review the documents and ensure they are up to date for the upcoming move.

When a student arrives at a new school, it is helpful to have documentation already in hand to support the child's need for services. Lacking documentation could result in a longer wait for evaluations and assistance, while the receiving school makes a determination about services. This could delay or have a negative impact on learning.

RESEARCH SCHOOL CHOICES

Military families are faced with education choices each time they move, such as:

- Public school in the home district, open enrollment in an outside district, charter and magnet schools, or online public school

- DoDEA school or DoDEA Virtual High School

- Private school, with or without religious affiliation

- Home school, with or without a co-op

- Specialized programs, such as dual enrollment, language immersion, or International Baccalaureate

Some families make different choices at different times in a child's school career, sometimes even different choices for the differing needs of children within the same family. Sometimes, a student may combine options, for example, supplementing home school with selected classes at a public or private school.

PARENT POINTER

School options and choices may vary with each move. Using an **Education Binder** helps keep students on track for course placement, advancement, and graduation requirements, from school to school as well as types of schooling, such as a homeschooled student re-entering public school.

For public schools, important information about school priorities, planning, and spending are found in public records like school board meeting minutes. At any school, a conversation with a guidance counselor may yield details about course offerings and more. School liaison officers can answer some questions about schools near their military installation, as well as homeschool requirements.

Military families in the target location can offer their perspectives, but more than one opinion is advisable. One positive or negative experience may not reflect the quality of the entire program.

LOOK FOR DIFFERING STANDARDS

Education standards vary widely between states. Before a move, review grade-level standards for the receiving state to gain insight into what challenges a student could face in the classroom after a move. Parents and teachers can then discuss whether the student is lacking in any skills needed in a new location. This communication can give students a better chance for a smoother transition into a new curriculum.

Stacy's children attended school in Texas for two years, then transferred to Ohio. Ohio had adopted Common Core curriculum, but Texas had not. Stacy did not find that either state standard was deficient, but they were different enough to cause some academic struggles for both her children. After a few months of extra time and attention to homework and a determination to keep a positive attitude, Stacy's children were able to tackle the change and embrace it. Stacy's takeaway from this experience was a determination to do more research into the curriculum of new schools before the next move.

Knowing about curriculum differences ahead of time gives the student-advocacy team time to prepare the student for the change. That preparation could save weeks of frustration at a new school.

Academic assessments, if possible, should also take curriculum requirements at the receiving school into consideration. If the team determines the student needs more support than classroom work, practice, or tutoring can provide, they may consider referral services. The earlier these assessments are made, the more time the student has to address areas of concern.

PLAN PROJECTS AND EXAMS

As part of the exit plan, the student-advocacy team should prioritize upcoming projects and exam schedules. The student may need to submit projects or take exams early to give a teacher time to grade and return material before the student leaves, if departure doesn't coincide with the end of the school year.

Particularly for high school students, projects and major tests fill the final weeks of school. If a move is happening in conjunction with the end of the school year, it becomes especially important for the student to plan ahead and create a timeline for accomplishing important end-of-year tasks. Also, student and parents will need to set aside any needed materials if household goods will be packed before the project is complete.

PARENT POINTER

Ask a prospective school:

› What are the dates for registration and the first day of school?

› Does the school require local health certificates or additional immunizations?

› What paperwork is required for enrollment?

› What evaluations for special programs and services can be completed ahead?

› When are sign-ups or tryouts for clubs and sports?

› What are the requirements for transferring credits and graduation?

› Are there summer reading lists or project requirements?

When orders are in hand, the anticipated move becomes reality. When parents and teachers have paved the way for the transition with good planning and solid communication, the exit plan assures a smooth transition.

DOCUMENTATION

As the exit plan progresses, the team will add necessary documentation and notes, ensuring the student's Education Binder is up to date, bursting with work samples, report cards, and teacher communications.

Teachers and parents should review together a student's social and academic strengths and weaknesses, discussing any notable areas of achievement or concern. This is a good time to confirm a student is on track for success.

When students transition within the same school system, teachers often communicate personally across grade levels about the strengths and challenges of their students. For example, ninth grade teachers talk to both eighth grade and tenth grade teachers to ensure academic alignment across

BINDER BUILDER

A **teacher-to teacher letter** introduces a student's abilities and personality including:

> Academic strengths and weaknesses

> Areas of growth

> Behavior and peer relationships

> Learning style

> Character and demeanor

> Seating preferences

> Enrichment or support services the student may need

> Hobbies, sports, or clubs the student enjoys

Teacher-to-teacher letters in high school can also be the basis for letters of recommendation for college and other applications. Consider asking key teachers as early as ninth grade for letters of recommendation to use in the future. Keeping in contact with mentors and significant adults is a good practice for students for many reasons, including maintaining key relationships for future recommendations.

grade levels. A military student in transition from one school to another will not benefit from this level of connection. However, a teacher-to-teacher letter, describing the student's personality, strengths, and particular needs, can serve the same purpose.

A letter from one teacher may be enough, particularly for elementary students, or parents and students may request letters from various teachers, counselors, or coaches. For high schoolers, a letter from all core teachers is a good idea. These letters can detail academic strengths and needs, as well as extracurricular interests and talents. The purpose is to help receiving teachers facilitate the student's transition into new classrooms and school environments.

Academics aren't the only area where continuity can be lost. Teacher-to-teacher letters can describe a student's leadership roles, volunteerism, and work ethic to help paint a picture of the student for new teachers who would not know the student's history otherwise. These letters may help provide a basis for membership in competitive clubs and activities.

> **PARENT POINTER**
>
> The last few weeks of school are busy for teachers as well as the family who is moving. Parents should ask teachers and counselors for letters or other personalized material for the Education Binder as early in the school session as possible. Even if a move is not coming, letters from teachers are valuable binder material.

EMOTIONS AND REACTIONS

When a move is on the horizon, it is normal for military-connected students to feel a range of emotions, from excitement about a new adventure, to sadness over leaving friends and familiar places, or even anger at the circumstances of a parent's military career. Grief is also a common response. Individual reactions about a move will vary—sometimes from one day to the next—depending on personalities, support systems, and previous transition experiences.

Allowing children to express their grief, anger, happiness, or other feelings about a move is healthy and keeps channels of communication open, even if all conversations are not positive.

Expecting children to suppress their feelings is more likely to close those channels.

> *Kristin and her family were scheduled to move again in a month. They had moved every year for the past three years. Kristin's daughter, Sienna, was just shy of her tenth birthday. She had never lived anywhere longer than twenty-three months, and this would be her eighth move in her nine-plus years of life. She had made good friends in her current home. Sienna liked her school and her teachers, too. Kristin made the new place sound as exciting as possible without overselling it. At the same time, Kristin gave Sienna permission to hate everything about the move for the first few weeks after she received the news.*

Moving is difficult. Students may experience apprehension about leaving the known for the unknown, and may have a confusing mixture of positive and negative feelings about the move. When parents talk about their own feelings, students may feel less alone and become exposed to new ways of thinking about the situation. It's important to remember to encourage students to express their enthusiasm if they are looking forward to a move.

> *Megan, a high school student, says each of her moves was an opportunity for adventure. Some of her friends also found moving exciting, an opportunity to change their hair color, adopt a new nickname, or recreate themselves in other ways. Other friends did not respond so well. "One friend who rode the bus with me refused to shower starting the day her family received orders to move. She said she would shower when her dad canceled the move. It was a small bus and a big smell," Megan recalls.*

Strong emotions may result in behavior changes. Parents and teachers must discern what forms of expression are

Teacher-to-teacher letters can describe a student's leadership roles, volunteerism, and work ethic to help paint a picture of the student for new teachers who would not know the student's history otherwise.

acceptable and which are not, perhaps enlisting the help of a counselor. Whatever the emotions associated with a move, the student will be better able to process them when she can express them in healthy ways. When other family members also share their feelings, recognizing that each person may have different thoughts about the same move, they can support each other and create stronger bonds.

SOCIAL GOODBYE

It's important for a military-connected student to have opportunities for closure and to say goodbye to classmates, friends, and other special people in their lives. As the departure date approaches, parents and teachers should tune in to what the student is saying through verbal and nonverbal cues.

The act of saying goodbye is an important and healthy step in transition, even if it is sometimes painful. It is important for both the student who is leaving and the friends remaining. Encourage students to say goodbye in the way they are most comfortable, whether they prefer to do so quietly to individuals or to an entire class.

Parents can't stop children from experiencing hurt or grief, but they can help them navigate their emotions in a healthy way. Teachers, counselors, coaches, doctors, and friends can be invited to the team in the final weeks before a move, to help the student stay engaged and feel important to the community.

One way to ease the transition is to talk about creative ways to stay in touch. Use technology old and new. Give students a place to collect addresses, emails, phone numbers, and social media handles as appropriate.

Students may wish to stay in touch with teachers as well as peers. Many military kids refer to their past teachers during the

PARENT POINTER

When preparing to say goodbye, children may want to talk about what they will miss about the home they are leaving or may want to make a list of things to do before it's time to say goodbye. Consider a reasonable plan for visiting favorite places one more time or inviting close friends for one more sleepover. Take photos and capture final moments to help children say goodbye with few regrets.

new school year saying things like, "I wish Ms. Avery could see how great my cursive is now," or "I wonder how Ms. Timmons is doing, I miss her." These are signs of a great teacher. Staying in touch with key educators helps children feel grounded and connected to their personal history.

These connections also reinforce positive experiences for teachers when they see the results of investment in a military-connected student, even after a move. Occasional updates from former students give teachers concrete examples of the value of caring for military-connected students.

While Emily was stationed overseas, she was so proud to create a video in Venice for her previous Italian teacher. It was a short video simply thanking the teacher for teaching her the language. In class, Emily thought she would never have the opportunity to use Italian, but after traveling to Italy and practicing her language skills, Emily could not wait to reach back to her teacher to say thank you.

TEACHER TIP

Party! Whether it's cupcakes in class, a bowling party, swim party, or day at the park, allow time for a student to say goodbye to friends and teachers.

Plant a garden. Let students plant flowers or a tree together as a friendship garden. Even after the military-student moves away, the friendship garden remains. Students who are not moving may be sad about losing the friend who is moving. A friendship garden is for the friends who stay, as much as the one who is leaving.

Take a class picture. Mount a picture on card stock or construction paper for each student, and have all the students sign each one or write short notes. When the student moves away, she will always have the sweet picture and notes from friends.

Create pen pals. Military kids make great classroom pen pals. Consider real mail, email, or video chats as a way to stay in touch and talk about different states or different cultures in other countries.

ACADEMIC GOODBYE

Just as friends might start pulling away and emotionally disconnecting before a move, a student who is moving may begin to disconnect academically. Like withdrawing socially, this is a coping mechanism to disconnect before the move. It could also be a reaction to the chaos of moving. Rooms may be boxed up. Families may be in temporary quarters. All these factors detract from the ability to focus and give consistent attention to school work. This is a critical time to help the student finish strong.

At home, create a study area suitable for completing homework. If home is in disarray, as it often must be during preparations for a move, consider another place for students to focus on homework, perhaps at the library or a friend's house. Teachers can also provide additional study time in the classroom before or after school.

In the classroom, reconsider homework requirements. If it becomes obvious to someone on the student-advocacy team—including the student—that school work is becoming overwhelming, the team should discuss and assess the homework load together. Be sure that all homework is necessary for the student's mastery of the material. Time is precious in the lead-up to a major transition. Parents and students should not be hesitant to ask teachers for some leeway. Teachers should be willing to consider adjustments to homework requirements, based on a particular student's educational and emotional needs.

Ms. Branch, who teaches tenth grade history, agrees that homework expectations can be adjusted before a move, as long as students provide work that shows mastery of the subject. She works closely with families getting ready to move to determine if the home situation can continue to handle homework. Ms. Branch says a partially-completed classroom assignment shows her more about a student's learning than hastily completed homework done amid the confusion of packing for a move.

In his first grade class, Mr. Garcia stops nightly homework for students who are moving. He believes accomplishments in the classroom can assess student knowledge as efficiently as homework. If a student needs added practice to gain a critical skill before moving, Mr. Garcia partners with the parent to determine the best way to support the child's learning.

Structure is still important, but schedules and needs will begin to change as the move draws closer. Establish routines that accommodate changing circumstances, and maintain them as much as possible. Open communication keeps everyone aware of changes as they occur.

The student-advocacy team should set positive expectations. Moving occurs often in the life of a military child, and it's important to develop good skills to manage transition. If moving woes are accepted as excuses for lack of attention to school work or unacceptable behavior, those behaviors will become part of the cycle. Meltdowns will occasionally happen, but parents and teachers should still expect positive behavior and attention to studies.

Summer slide, the term for learning that is lost during school break, is a concern for all students. Military-connected students may experience this slide during the summer or during any gap caused by transition, and it may have more impact when a move happens during the school year.

Teachers can mitigate the effects of transition by giving students appropriate assignments to work on during transition, including some that address any known areas of

CONVERSATION

Parent to teacher

› How can we help my child say goodbye to the class?

› Who can we talk to if my child is having a difficult time adjusting?

› What can we do during transition to reduce lost learning?

› Are there any skills that should be assessed upon arrival by the new teacher?

needed development. Teachers at the sending school can give assignments from the current location and parents can reach out to the receiving school to ask for a list of homework the student will need to complete to be on level with classmates. A reading list will help maintain reading skills at the appropriate level.

Military students can take this work on the road and gain confidence by practicing their skills. Parents recognize these tools may keep their children active and engaged, a positive distraction during travel and down time, when kids have little to do but stare at electronic screens or out windows.

DEPARTURE

In the weeks leading up to departure, students should continue extracurricular activities as much as possible. Finishing the soccer season, participating in a music recital or school play, or attending a spring dance, will provide necessary closure and connection with friends. In the classroom, allow a student to participate fully in classroom activities.

A carefully executed exit plan accomplishes the tasks of transition in a timely manner, leaving to the end only the details that cannot be completed earlier.

DEPARTURE LIST FOR PARENTS

- Request official records from the current school. As soon as an address is available for the receiving school, request that records be sent there.

- Obtain copies of student records and transcripts for the Education Binder. The Interstate Compact provides for the sending school to allow records to be hand carried and for the receiving school to allow provisional enrollment until official records are received from the previous school. Not all schools are aware of these provisions, making it essential for parents to be familiar with them.

Moving occurs often in the life of a military child, and it's important to develop good skills to manage transition. If moving woes are accepted as excuses for lack of attention to school work or unacceptable behavior, those behaviors will become part of the cycle.

- If a new school has been selected, make advance appointments with the receiving school to smooth the process of enrollment, course selection and placement, and any needed evaluations. Request schedules for extracurricular tryouts and opportunities to connect with coaches, band directors, and other activity leaders of interest.

- Arrange for the student to say goodbye to key teachers and friends. The busyness of a move can be all consuming, but students and families need opportunities for closure.

DEPARTURE LIST FOR TEACHERS

- Offer students a packet of assignments, activities, and worksheets to help maintain academic skills during travel and transition, or a larger packet if the move happens during summer break.

- Provide teacher-to-teacher communication, and other material requested for the Education Binder, to provide a more complete picture of the student.

- Make time to say a personal goodbye to the student. Allow time for classmates to do so as well, in a way that fits the student's wishes.

As the Season of Leaving comes to a close, departing students and parents may feel lonely and sad, as they say goodbye to familiar friends, places, and routines. But this season is also a time of excitement, as they dream of all the possibilities that come with a new school, neighborhood, and home.

SEASON OF
ARRIVING

Getting ready for the first day at a new school ushers in the Season of Arriving. In this season, the student-advocacy team prepares the student for a new school environment and prepares the new school for the student. The season begins while the family is transitioning to a new location and continues through registration, the first day of school, and initial parent-teacher conferences, where the student-advocacy team can get a first read on how the new student is adjusting.

The United States military moves hundreds of thousands of service members and their families every year. More than half of those moves are during the months of May through August. Moves that align with the school cycle are ideal, when the move takes place over the summer break and the student's first day at a new school is also the first day of the school year.

Sometimes, the Season of Arriving begins at winter break or in the middle of a semester. Sometimes the disparity between school end and start dates from one school to another can create issues, even for summer moves.

In all these situations, thorough preparation during the Season of Leaving sets up the student for success in this Season of Arriving. A well-stocked Education Binder provides the new school with a holistic history of the military-connected student, allowing for a smooth integration into a new school environment.

TRANSITION

On both ends of a move, a military family may spend days or weeks in hotels or sleeping on the floor of an empty house surrounded by boxes. This sense of homelessness—although temporary—has implications for the student's ability to participate in school and begin to connect in a new community.

If a family has not yet established residency in a desired school district, students may be delayed in enrollment, as well as miss sports tryouts or registration for extracurricular activities. This is especially frustrating when the family is already in the area, stuck in limbo until a lease or purchase agreement is signed.

All moves have some level of difficulty no matter how many times a family has moved. Complicating factors include relocating to and from overseas locations, living in temporary housing while looking for a home to buy or rent, or waiting for housing to become available on a military installation. Families waiting for military housing are usually put on a waiting list, and upward movement on the list is unpredictable.

> A well-stocked Education Binder provides the new school with a holistic history of the military-connected student, allowing for a smooth integration into a new school environment.

Jake and his family moved to Hawaii two weeks after the school year began. While the family waited for a house to become available on base, they lived in a hotel on the military installation. The school serving students in the military housing area, recognizing the difficulty of their situation, honored the hotel lodging verification as proof of residence. The school allowed Jake's family a forty-five-day grace period in which to find a home within the school boundaries—on base. If the family did not get a house within forty-five days, the children would no longer be eligible to be enrolled in the school. The family anxiously awaited a phone call from the military housing office. Finally, on day forty-three, they were offered a house. They took it, allowing the children to remain in school.

Transition issues can even affect the annual ritual of buying school supplies. A family may have to put off completing purchases until they know where their children will attend school, and therefore which supply list to consult. Sometimes the arrival or unpacking of household goods is delayed, and favorite backpacks, pencils, or folders may be impossible or difficult to find. These details may seem small, but they can add to the frustration of a school transition.

Every move is different, whether a military family moves to a neighboring state or to another country. After long drives, flight delays, lost luggage, family vacations squeezed into the chaos of moving, and perhaps a period of homelessness, the military-connected student is finally ready to register at the new school.

School start dates range from the beginning of August in some states to the beginning of September in others. Some districts are year-round, others traditional, still others— particularly secondary schools—follow a trimester system. This complicates a relocation when the semesters or trimesters of the sending and receiving schools do not match up.

When Stacy was moving from Germany back to the United States, she realized the end of the school year at her kids' DoDEA school in mid-June and the start of their receiving school in Florida in early August left a tight window for the move. Moving from overseas usually means waiting several weeks for household goods to arrive stateside. Stacy realized her family would possibly still be homeless and living out of suitcases on the first day of school.

In those chaotic weeks, in addition to finding and establishing a home, the family would have to manage placement tests for classes, find a health care provider to administer physicals needed for school registration, and attend soccer tryouts.

Knowing the calendar ahead of time allowed Stacy's family to plan accordingly. They knew their shipment would not arrive before the first day of school, so they packed school supplies and math workbooks in their suitcases, along with clothes, shoes, and soccer cleats.

Stacy also carried her children's Education Binders with all school documents, test results, reading levels, up-to-date physicals, shot records, work samples, and more to be ready for school registration.

REGISTRATION

After establishing residency, whether permanent or provisional, parents can schedule an appointment with the receiving school to complete the registration process and meet with the person responsible for placing the student in appropriate classes. After classes are assigned, parents and students may request to meet with individual teachers or team teachers, as needed. This is also a good time to follow up on any introductions that were made long distance during the Season of Leaving.

During the process of registration and class placement, various materials in the Education Binder will be instrumental at different times and appointments. Depending on the preference of the school or parents, portions of the binder or copies of specific pages can be presented.

BINDER BUILDER

Create a table of contents and tabs for each category of information in the Education Binder to keep track of what is in the binder and how to access it easily.

✐ **At registration**: Necessary documents may include shot records, birth certificate, school physical verification, and unofficial transcripts, if official records are not yet available.

✐ **For class placement**: Depending on the age of the student, this meeting might be with a guidance counselor or an administrator. Helpful materials include active education plans, standardized test results, work samples, sequential report cards, the student's academic preferences for honors or advance placement subjects, and applicable documentation showing eligibility for special programs.

✎ **At initial meetings with classroom teachers**: Teacher-to-teacher letters, including information about any classroom environment needs, and lists of books and content covered in previous courses. If the student has particular needs or requirements, parents can outline strategies that have worked for them and for other teachers.

The student-advocacy team for elementary students comes together when the student and parents meet the classroom teacher or teachers. They will form the core of support for the student.

For secondary students, the student-advocacy team is larger. It will include the guidance counselor, who will help with class placement and will usually be the point person for overall student health and adjustment. After the class schedule is assigned, parents and the student may ask for meetings with individual teachers as necessary, who will also become part of the team. This is a good time to set up a high school student for self-advocacy, learning procedures and key contacts for help with day-to day concerns, big or small.

Initial communication is important for creating the student-advocacy team, whether the student arrives at the beginning of the school year or after classes have begun. Educators should ask specifically about the student's academic and personal history, including the number of moves and past schools, and possible upcoming family separations or deployments.

Registration and enrollment are the best times for schools to share information about school procedures and policies, and for the parents to pass along any pertinent details about the provisions of the Interstate Compact and, if necessary, provide a copy of the compact to an administrator or counselor.

Actions to consider at registration or before:

- Parents may wish to speak to a grade level teacher or counselor for an indication of the climate of the school and programs available to students.

- Parents will want to know how parent-teacher conferences are structured and scheduled.

- Secondary students should receive clear information about transferring credits, graduation requirements, class ranking, and how to determine appropriate placement in academic classes.

- Secondary students should take note of upcoming test dates for PSAT, SAT, or ACT, as well as any state-mandated tests they may not be familiar with yet.

PREPARE THE STUDENT FOR THE FIRST DAY

The first day of school for a military-connected student is the official arrival of the student into a new school, regardless of the school's calendar. Successful transitions are directly related to successful preparation, yet even with preparation, the process of beginning at a new school fills a student's mind with questions like:

> *Will my teacher like me?*
> *Will I understand math?*
> *Will I have good friends in my class?*

With every move and new school, military kids have additional questions that come with starting over—again:

> *Who will I sit with at lunch?*
> *How long will I be here?*
> *Will we stay here if my parent deploys?*

The Season of Arriving includes many new experiences and is often stressful and tiring. It is the season of throwing off old routines and adopting new ones. Everyone involved in the uprooted family experiences the transition, yet feels very different emotions.

When entering a new school, students must adjust to a new environment. They establish new peer groups, meet new teachers, learn new school rules and procedures, find new support systems, clubs, sports, and other activities.

Parents are unpacking a new house, settling into a new job and community, balancing their own integration into the community, and working to ensure all vital records are transferred—school, medical, dental—from the previous location to the new one.

A parent may be as overwhelmed as a student, but it's important to make time—amid the flurry of paperwork—to prepare the student for the first day of school. Often, a first day of school involves new clothes, new school supplies, and a return to a school routine or learning a new one. A little extra preparation goes a long way toward a good transition:

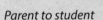

CONVERSATION

Parent to student

› What makes you happy about our new town?

› What will you miss the most about our old neighborhood?

› Is there anything you won't miss?

› What seems scary about this move?

› What's the best thing about this move?

› When a student's first day at a new school is also the first day of school for other students, connect with families who have students of similar ages and make plans to get together, ideally before school starts. Knowing one or two familiar faces on the first day of school is invaluable, particularly if those students are new too.

› Talk about questions, concerns, fears, or excitement about this new adventure to help set the student's mind at ease. Allow the student to express frustration, sadness, or anger, as well as joy.

- Attend orientation or visit the school before the first day of class to help the student get to know the environment and where to find core areas such as classrooms, cafeteria, gym, nurse, and the counselor's office.

- Get a map of the school as well as bus and class schedules ahead of time so the student can plot routes and schedules.

- For students arriving after the school year has begun, consider attending class for the first time on a Thursday or Friday. This allows the student to get acclimated before starting a full week of classes.

PREPARE THE CLASSROOM

Every student contributes to the dynamic of the classroom, each one bringing personal experiences, perspectives, learning styles, and communication preferences. As a new student prepares for the first day in a brand new school environment, the environment should be prepared as well.

Teachers can use carefully-chosen books, games, and seating charts to make sure a classroom is welcoming and ready for the arrival of new students. The challenge is not only for military-connected students to adapt, but also for the class and classroom to adapt and accept newcomers, making them part of the classroom team.

Just as parents have their checklists to prepare their child for the first day of school, teachers have their own checklists to prepare for new students and to create an effective learning environment. Teachers prepare for the first school day by reviewing curriculum, decorating classrooms, getting supplies, creating seating charts, and more.

A few adjustments to a teacher's planning can help new military-connected students acclimate into a classroom. No matter when a student arrives, these additions can help ease the transition:

🖉 **Welcome packet**: A school welcome packet may include a map of the school, the schedule and calendar, and a student handbook. Teachers can tailor content based on the student's interests, providing information about the classroom and community.

🖉 **Extra supplies**: A starter kit of classroom supplies for newcomers can make the difference between a comfortable first day and a traumatic one. Keep core supplies—paper, pens, pencils, folders, composition notebooks, ruler, calculator— available for a new student to borrow in the first days. The lack of a writing utensil shouldn't be the cause of a rocky experience in a new class.

> **TEACHER TIP**
>
> Use information gained from initial meetings to customize a welcome packet for a new student. This can become a springboard for the next conversation with the student and parents.

🖉 **Buddy system**: Buddies can show new students around campus and sit with them at lunch. If the school does not have a buddy program, teachers can create one for their classes. The system can be more formal for younger students, and informal for older ones. For older students, rather than call it a buddy system, teachers may ask a classmate to help a new student find the cafeteria, or connect students with similar interests in casual conversation during class.

🖉 **Ice breakers**: Word games and conversation starters for the class will help students get to know one another, especially new classmates.

🖉 **Integrated roles**: If a class has a rotating list of classroom helpers, or a birthday list, a new student should be included right away. This inclusion helps the student integrate with classmates more quickly.

🖉 **Open seats**: If a classroom has assigned seats, a few available desks sprinkled throughout the room provide a better welcome to new students. When a new student joins the classroom at any time during the school year, it's nice to offer a seat surrounded by classmates, rather than an isolated, leftover desk in the back row.

✎ **Warm welcome**: Educators can remind established students of any age to welcome new students. The teacher may designate meeting places where new students can connect with others throughout the day. A little extra effort from a teacher can ensure the student understands nuances in a school, from the simple (bathroom locations) to complex (school dress codes), especially for students arriving after the start of the school year who may have missed orientation.

✎ **Good books**: Military-connected students will appreciate books that relate to their needs and experiences. These books will also prove to be interesting to classmates, helping introduce them to military life. Many books about military life are available for different grades and reading levels. MilitaryFamilyBooks.com carries quality fiction and nonfiction books about military life, for children and adults, from a variety of publishers.

✎ **New-parent support**: Teachers can connect new parents with a parent who knows the school and routine. Providing this connection is part of the communication that will solidify the student-advocacy relationship of parent and teacher.

The teacher doesn't bear the entire responsibility for helping students make friends, but can establish a safe and welcoming environment for all students. An atmosphere conducive to friendship development plays a key role in positive classroom atmosphere, healthy student behavior, and preventing bullying.

TEACHER TIP

"Please don't assess me my first day in class. I want to meet people. I want to make friends. I can't do that if I'm taking a test all day long."

Mr. Adams says he gives a new student time for a social welcome before beginning academic assessments. He makes sure the student is part of class discussions and projects and finds a lunch buddy on that crucial first day. Assessments can begin on Day 2, still allowing time for the new student to socialize and integrate into the classroom.

In an article from the Harvard Graduate School of Education, Dr. Mary Keller, president of MCEC notes that the first two weeks at a new school are crucial for military-connected students. "What we know about moving and changing schools is that there's an urgency there," she said. "Consistently, our research shows that you've got about two weeks when a kid is new to a school to help him fit it. We call it the fragile first two weeks."

KEEP AN EYE ON EMOTIONS

After the first day is past and the new military-connected student begins to integrate into the new school environment, it's important for the student-advocacy team to be intentional about assessing the social and emotional landscape surrounding the student. Before a new student can acclimate and succeed academically, he must first adjust emotionally, which usually involves integrating into the social environment.

The military-connected student may still be grieving the loss of friendships and a previous home. The student has just left her established social environment and community of teachers and friends. It can take a while to establish trust and develop a new support system.

The student-advocacy team should communicate about any adjustment issues, even before it's time for parent-teacher conferences. Depending on the issues at hand, the team may wish to meet in person. The student-advocacy team should share what they have observed about the student's behavior, as well as any academic concerns that show up in the student's classwork, homework, or early evaluations.

Ms. Schmidt teaches fourth graders in a DoDEA school overseas, where many of her students have moved frequently and where she has many new students every year. During the first two weeks of school, Ms. Schmidt watches her students carefully to see which students sit

"You've got about two weeks when a kid is new to a school to help him fit it. We call it the fragile first two weeks."

together at lunch, walk to class, and play together on the playground. She looks for signs of social well-being early in the school year, after the arrival of a new student, and always before scheduled parent-teacher conferences. The students are unaware their teacher is watching to see whether new students are welcomed and included, or if they have to make their own inroads into a group of friends. She also watches to see if new students are making wise decisions about behavior and choosing friends.

In addition to watching friend interactions at lunch and recess, a teacher may watch to see how and when a student interacts with classmates, raises her hand or participates in class, and whether she has a friend in the classroom. Each of these social checks may be discussed by the student-advocacy team. If necessary, the team can design a plan to help the child develop strong healthy friendships.

ASSESS CLASS AND COURSE PLACEMENT

Differing state standards for all types of education programs create recurring frustrations for military-connected students, from kindergarten start dates to high school graduation requirements, to course placement.

CONVERSATION

Teacher to student

› What about this school is different from your last school? What is the same?

› What were your mascot and school colors at your last school?

› What was your favorite thing to do where you used to live? What did you do after school?

› So far, what is your favorite thing here in your new home or school?

Teacher to parent

› How many times have you moved?

› How do you think your student is handling this move?

› How is this different from other moves?

› What can I do to support your student?

The provisions of the Interstate Compact help the student-advocacy team recognize fulfilled graduation requirements and ensure some continuity for course placement.

If a student qualified for a particular program at a previous school, advanced placement classes, or English as a second language, for example, the Interstate Compact allows the student to be placed in comparable classes in the receiving school without initial testing. The new school can then evaluate the student to ensure he has been placed accurately. This provision allows the student to continue a course of study rather than wait for evaluations.

For parents and students, knowing the programs and curricula offered at a receiving school and how they correspond to programs and curricula at the previous school will inform requests for course placement.

GIFTED, ACCELERATED, OR ENRICHED

Gifted and talented programs vary among school districts, so a student may be offered different options with each move. These variations may include:

- Enriched standard courses, such as an enriched version of the standard grade-level English class

- Pull-out programs or clusters, which allow small groups of students to temporarily leave the standard classroom environment to explore subjects in more depth

- Separate programs of study, which may group students of similar ability into separate classrooms or buildings and follow a separate curriculum

- Accelerated learning to another grade level, such as placing a fourth grade student in a fifth grade class for math or reading

- Immersion programs, such as core courses taught in a foreign language

- Alternate course options, such as a journalism course that replaces and satisfies the requirement of an English writing course

- After school and summer enrichment gifted programs, which help students develop new skills and enhance extraordinary learning capabilities

- Advanced Placement (AP), Postsecondary Enrollment Options (PSEO), College in the Schools (CIS), and similar courses that offer potential for both high school and college credits

While each of these may meet the need for a particular military-connected student at a particular time, potential exists for inconsistencies between programs that are not complementary or even compatible with one another. One gifted program may not prepare the student for a different program option at the next school.

When David entered public school for the first time, the gifted program at his school was an enrichment of standard curricula, rather than a separate program of study.

At his next school, when he became disruptive, his teacher realized David was extremely bored and suggested a different path for him. His student-advocacy team redesigned his studies, putting him in a higher grade for math and reading. After testing, the school psychologist eventually suggested a full grade acceleration.

At David's third public school, there was no program for accelerated learning above grade level in math or reading. Instead, teachers were encouraged to go "deeper and wider" within a subject, which meant an occasional extra sheet of math work. The only supplemental programs were an after-school math activity for all levels and an independent computer program David could work on when he finished his math work.

It is frustrating for a military family when a student's academic needs go unmet, and it can be problematic for a teacher as well. If the problem is not one that can be alleviated by the Interstate Compact, the student-advocacy team may need to develop other strategies.

A busy teacher may not have the time or resources to design a special program for a child with different learning abilities, but parents and students have options. If a class or program is unavailable in a particular area, a student can explore subjects independently or focus on areas in need of improvement. Online programs, homeschool curricula, and additional reading can supplement classroom material. Also consider age-appropriate community courses or extracurricular activities outside of school, which can cover interests as broad as fiction writing, robotics, and politics.

Sometimes, for military-connected students, the problem is the availability and timeliness of school assessment for programs. In that case, parents may have the option to get outside testing for a student.

MAXIMIZE THE FIRST CONFERENCE

At the first parent-teacher conference, the student-advocacy team begins to coalesce. This is a good time to intentionally assess the student's initial class placement, academic work, and social adjustment to the new environment. All members of the team, including the student as appropriate, should come prepared to ask questions about assessments, education plans, previous experiences, classroom procedures, and any other topics of concern.

If, at a prior meeting, the team was able to discuss strategies that worked for the student in the past, the first conference is a good time to review those strategies and assess their efficiency. A new teacher will have new ideas and different approaches as well. It's important for all members of the team to listen to one another's perspectives.

Student involvement in these discussions is also helpful. This is particularly true for secondary students, but elementary students can also take part in parent-teacher conferences in age-appropriate ways. For example, a student can show and discuss current work with a parent or show work from a previous school to a new teacher.

Questions and topics for team members to discuss or review at the first parent-teacher conference might include:

- Is the student comfortable with his peers? Does he spend time with friends at lunch or recess?

- What is her demeanor in class? Is she comfortable participating in discussions and projects?

- Does he appear to be ahead or behind in the current curriculum? If there is a gap or overlap, what strategies can be used to address it?

- What are the student's academic and personal goals? How can the team help her work toward those goals?

- What special programs has the student been involved in at previous schools?

- How many schools has the student attended and where has he lived?

- What extracurricular activities does she enjoy and hope to continue?

- Are there any upcoming or anticipated deployments or other family separations?

This meeting also provides an opportunity to review material in the Education Binder that may be pertinent. Any notes from the meeting should be added to the binder for future reference.

If the usual time set aside for parent-teacher meetings is too brief to address all the questions related to a new student, the student-advocacy team may consider making an additional or extended appointment to continue the conversation. As the student is settling in to the new environment, it's essential for the team to be sure any curriculum discrepancies or social adjustment difficulties are recognized and addressed. If any member of the team is concerned that unresolved issues may be unrelated to transition, the earlier those are recognized the better. This first conference may be a good time to discuss the possibility of testing for special programs of any kind.

The Season of Arriving is a crucial time. The student-advocacy team comes together. The student is placed in appropriate classes and begins to acclimate to the landscape of a new school. It's a season of many challenges, and good communication between team members is essential, as is persistence. By using some of the tools of cultivation—the helpful provisions of the Interstate Compact and a well-stocked Education Binder—the team can establish a strong foundation for success at a new school.

SEASON OF
GROWING

In the Season of Growing, the transplanted military-connected student begins to put down roots in a new school and begins to grow among a group of peers, academically and personally. During this season, the primary focus is on making sure the student's learning is on target.

Standards, calendars, and curricula vary from school to school, which may cause a student to experience a gap or overlap in learning opportunities. Early in this growing season, the student-advocacy team will note any struggles the student may have and discern the cause: curriculum alignment, personal adjustment, or learning ability.

This is also a season for nurturing healthy friendships and good study habits. Community involvement is helpful for both parents and students, as volunteer and extracurricular activities create connections and opportunities for relationships. These connections promote growth across support networks, as well as the flow of communication between home, school, and student.

MIND THE GAP AND THE OVERLAP

All states are not equal when it comes to expectations, grading policies, and learning objectives. Students in the same grades but different states may learn vastly different material. A major academic challenge of military-connected students when they move from school to school is the potential for mismatched curricula and a patchwork of content standards. The student in a new classroom may be either ahead or behind her new classmates, or ahead in some subjects and behind in others. All these variables can hamper learning progress and continuity.

Cooperation on the student-advocacy team is necessary to address these issues, because the solutions must be matched to the individual student and across all subjects. Particularly for secondary students, it's possible the same student could have gaps in some classes and overlaps in others.

For example, if a high school student arrives in his new literature class just in time to study *Romeo and Juliet*—again—perhaps he could study another Shakespeare tragedy and compare and contrast the two for additional understanding. On the other hand, the student might welcome the review in literature, while tackling missed units in algebra.

Meeting each student's needs appropriately requires close communication between the student, teachers, and parents, to ensure the student continues learning and advancing, rather than being confused or bored. For all members of the team, communication about the requirements in all subjects is essential to determine the path to take.

> Students in the same grades but different states may learn vastly different material.

Aimee changed schools in the middle of her fifth grade year. Her previous school had ten spelling words a week; her new school had twenty-five words plus definitions. At her previous school, she was beginning to learn the locations of the fifty US states. Her new school had already learned about twenty-five states, which were incorporated into lessons, with the expectation that students could place the states on a map, spell each correctly, and label the state capitals. Aimee quickly went from being an A student to failing both spelling and geography. The teacher realized the curriculum was the same but the expectations were

*very different. Aimee's teacher met with her parents, and
they agreed on a gradual plan to bring Aimee up to the
same proficiency as her peers. The first week, Aimee would
learn twelve of the twenty-five spelling words, fourteen the
next week until she learned all twenty-five. Similarly, in
geography, Aimee would be tested on five states at a time,
until she caught up with the class.*

Time and attention from the student-advocacy team can
reestablish academic progress and make up for missed steps in
the sequence of learning.

Sometimes repeated military moves—particularly if they
occur only a year apart—can create cumulative, growing
gaps in learning. Without careful attention, there's a risk the
military-connected student's needs will get lost in transition.
Perhaps he has not been at one school long enough for anyone
to recognize that an academic struggle—like reading below
grade level—is more than a transitional issue. By maintaining
and using an Education Binder, a parent can track the student's
learning and back up observations with evidence. If educational
progress has been well documented, the team can more easily
assess whether an academic issue is transitional or systemic.

*Ms. Cahill has military-connected students in her
high school classroom who are still reading at a third
grade level but not receiving support services. These
under-achieving students are flying under the radar. As a
military spouse herself, Ms. Cahill realizes these students'
challenges were probably noted and passed along as
transitional issues rather than continuing academic
needs. Or perhaps difficulties began in transition and grew
into continuing needs, because they were never addressed.
Sometimes the frequency of military moves means
the education system does not recognize or evaluate a
student's struggles in a timely way.*

Learning issues, even if they are transitional, need attention. Progress may be declining because of circumstances related to a move, or the problem may be an inability to grasp content. Either way, the student needs attention and assistance to address the problem. Careful attention should be given to the student's progress or lack thereof so that transitional difficulties don't become long-term learning issues.

As the student is getting established during the Season of Growing, if the advocacy team recognizes a struggle that persists beyond the first weeks in a new class, the next step is to assess whether the issue is alignment of curriculum, the student's personal adjustment, or the student's ability.

CURRICULUM ALIGNMENT

The teacher sees the student's present performance, while the parent and student are aware of past performance and experiences at a previous school. The teacher can find out if the new curriculum is ahead or behind the student's prior learning and experiences. Perhaps the curriculum is the same, but each school has approached it differently. Often, the student can advocate for herself, for example, explaining to a teacher that she has already completed a unit on fractions but has not been introduced to decimals. Conversations will highlight when a new teaching strategy is needed to help align the curriculum with the student's abilities and knowledge.

For missed academic content during a move, a student may need only a few minutes with the teacher each day—during lunch or after school—over the first few weeks. This undivided attention is one way to get the student up to speed in class, while also assessing progress. Spending a few minutes each day can prevent weeks of confusion and potential disruption in class. Busy work or repetition of material may cause the student to become bored and inattentive, missing out on new concepts integrated into familiar material.

> Careful attention should be given to the student's progress or lack thereof so that transitional difficulties don't become long-term learning issues.

The issue of misaligned curriculum can be addressed in other ways, too:

- Fellow students can team up to work with the new student. Some students will catch up quickly with guided peer support. As a bonus, working closely with peers gives the new student opportunities to make friends.

- The student may continue to use material learned in the previous school while transitioning to the new curriculum. For example, if the reading list from a former school is slightly different, the teacher could allow the student to use examples from books read in the previous school in class exams and essays. In this case, the student would be responsible for providing the teacher with a list of books read at the other school. Notes in the Education Binder will show what books and concepts the student has already covered and allow the new teacher to pair the learning material with what the student has already studied.

- Swapping the student to another class or teacher may be a better fit for both the student and teacher. Even in the same school, teachers cover material at varying paces. Perhaps the teacher in the room next door is teaching the unit at a higher level; or the teacher across the hall is covering a unit the student missed.

- If the student is ahead of classmates, he could become a tutor for struggling students, reinforcing the material he has already learned. Tutoring with supervision lets the teacher assess the student's understanding of the material.

PERSONAL ADJUSTMENT

When the curriculum is aligned, and a military-connected student is still struggling, the next thing to consider is the student's social and emotional adjustment to the new environment. Is the student having difficulty making friends or feeling at home in new surroundings? Is another military-life situation going on, such as a parent's deployment?

Every student of every age wants to belong, to have friends. When peer connections are lacking, the student may lose interest in school or have trouble focusing on studies. If a student is having difficulty integrating into a new school socially, the student-advocacy team may go back to strategies from the Season of Arriving, such as structured time to get to know peers or finding a new buddy.

The moment Jen walked into her third grade classroom in Virginia, she felt behind. Figuring out where to put her backpack and turn in homework caused her to miss the first few minutes of daily review, putting her out of sync for the entire day. After several more days of the same struggles, she lagged behind the class. After a week, she dissolved in a puddle of tears in class, revealing the emotional impact of her transition. The teacher immediately made Jen's mom aware of her daughter's sadness. Jen was longing for friends in her class, but because she was still struggling with the basics of classroom operation, she didn't have free time to meet new friends and socialize. Jen's sadness was rooted in her desire to make friends.

As a way to help Jen connect, the teacher started a girls-only lunch bunch in her classroom once a week to help the girls in the class get to know each other and Jen. The teacher also offered a boys-only lunch bunch, and on those days, the girls in the class sat together in the lunchroom, essentially creating two lunch bunch opportunities for both girls and boys each week. After the first lunch bunch, Jen felt cared for by both her teacher and her classmates.

Jen's elementary-school teacher, with kindness and creativity, helped her cultivate friendships. Encouraging friendships among middle school and high school students may require a different kind of tending. Preteens and teens are sometimes less willing to follow adult guidance when it comes to connecting with peers, but may respond to open invitations. Even for older students, a tuned-in student-advocacy team can find fertile ground for budding connections.

Amanda, while teaching high school, always started her morning with a cup of tea just before her first class. Students began asking if they could have a cup of tea as well. In response, Amanda created a weekly "Morning Tea with Ms. T," thirty minutes before first period. Each week, her classroom was full of students who came to school early, teacups in hand, to spend time with each other and their teacher. The morning ritual was a perfect opportunity for new students to get to know their classmates and for Amanda to spend time with her students.

At any grade level, the student-advocacy team can guide students toward supportive peer groups to create a sense of belonging. Matching a new student with others who have similar academic and extracurricular interests can help the student feel at home in a new school. For younger students, connecting a new student with a buddy sets up someone to sit with at lunch and play with at recess. For older students, parents and teachers may steer the student toward activities, clubs, and sports based on interests. Documenting past activities and successes in the Education Binder helps keep track of interests the student has explored and liked.

If any change in attitude or behavior causes concern to anyone on the student-advocacy team, it's important to share those concerns with the rest of the team. Parents are possibly unaware of the student's behavior in class. Teachers don't know the climate of life at home.

Communication is the foundation of a strong student-advocacy team. An email, phone call, or a note describing a tearful day or a good deed can make a difference. Keeping up to date on any changes—whether positive or negative—in behavior or performance is important. When the whole team is connected and aware, it's possible to find the underlying stressors and nip them in the bud before they grow into larger issues as the seasons march on.

When parents and teachers work together, they can support the student, develop strategies for improvement, and track progress of the student's adjustment.

ABILITY

Sometimes struggling in class goes beyond curriculum and adjusting to a new school. Sometimes poor academic performance is a symptom of another issue. If curriculum and adjustment have been addressed, and the student is still struggling by the first reporting period, the student-advocacy team should look for other possible causes of academic irregularities.

Emma missed the first two weeks of third grade because of a move. She started making friends, but her academic work didn't improve. Several weeks in, Emma's mom reached out to the teacher, concerned about her daughter's performance. A month into the school year, the teacher still suggested progress was slow because

TEAM TIP

Signs a student may still be having difficulty adjusting include:

› Changes in behavior at school or at home

› Lack of attention or participation in class

› Missing or incomplete assignments

› Not engaging in conversation with other students

› Spending more time alone than usual

*she missed the first two weeks of school. Emma's mom
pushed a little harder, believing transition was not the only
problem, and she was right. Further exploration revealed
borderline dyslexia, and appropriate strategies raised
Emma's performance and grades.*

For the military-connected student, if curriculum alignment
and adjustment issues have been ruled out, it is time to
consider other possibilities and pull in more support for the
student-advocacy team. The school guidance counselor should
be able to point the team in the right direction to assess the
situation and suggest strategies.

Actions may include tutoring plans, hearing and vision
tests, or assessment for a specialized education plan. The
sooner the situation is addressed, the sooner the student will
receive support and services. Adding documentation to the
Education Binder will improve continuing support after the
next move.

STUDENT INVOLVEMENT

One effective way for students to make friends and integrate
into a new school culture is through extracurricular activities.
Getting the student involved early in sports and clubs can
provide connection to peers with common interests.

Based on information in the Education Binder and
conversations with the student and parents, teachers can
recommend activities at the new school that fit the student's
interests.

- Share information from the student's Education Binder
  with new coaches or advisors, such as coach-to-coach
  or advisor-to-advisor letters, news articles about a
  student's performance or level of achievement, or copies
  of notable awards or recognitions.

- Make new students aware of signup timelines and let
  them know when other students—potential friends—

are joining a team or enrolling in an after-school program together.

The timing of a move may cause students to miss out on tryouts, eligibility, or information about participation in sports, clubs, and other activities.

Victoria faced obstacles when she wanted to try out for the school volleyball team her sophomore year in New Jersey. An experienced player, Victoria had played on volleyball teams in previous schools. At her new school, the district honored the Interstate Compact, which ensured Victoria would have the opportunity to try out for the team even though school tryouts had already taken place. However, the coach pulled Victoria aside and explained that although the compact guaranteed her a tryout, she would not make the team. Regardless of talent, the coach said he would not take a four-year lettering opportunity from a local student to give a spot on the team to a military-connected student who would leave after a year or two.

The Interstate Compact helps with some of these problems, but it can't resolve every situation. Military children may experience discrimination when they try out for athletic teams at a new school, or they may be welcomed with open arms.

According to the Interstate Compact, team application deadlines may be extended, but the team roster may be full before the military-connected student arrives. Tryouts in these situations may result in a wait list, but students are not guaranteed placement on the team.

In many situations, students are able to participate in their sport or activity of choice. Club sports and community activities offer additional opportunities. Still other students may choose to try something new at a new school, discovering pursuits that were not available at a previous school.

PARENT INVOLVEMENT

Involvement is a parent's key to understanding a new school and community. Teachers, schools, and local parents will appreciate the investment. Connecting in the civilian community shines a spotlight on both the challenges and advantages of military life.

School volunteering provides an inside source of information about a student's integration into a new school. Volunteering in the community or at school also gives military families a way to learn about local practices, systems, and processes.

Parents who work full or part time can still get involved and connect to the school. Parent-teacher groups, sports teams, and clubs often need volunteers on evenings and weekends. Parents do have busy schedules, and adding volunteerism may be taxing, but those hours are an investment in more than a team or event. No matter what time of day, volunteering gives parents another way to connect with the community, and with educators and other parents.

- **Parent-teacher groups**: Perhaps the best way to know the school and become an instant stakeholder is by joining the Parent Teacher Association or Parent Teacher Organization. Attend a few meetings; volunteer where slots are open. This affords opportunities for parents to connect with other parents and potentially the student's classmates for future social activities.

- **Classroom assistance**: For elementary school, there is rarely a teacher who doesn't need help in the classroom, from leading reading groups to decorating bulletin boards. Being in the classroom is a good way to see how a child interacts with peers as well with the teacher. In high school, volunteers are needed for theater productions, school dances, and team booster clubs.

Taking on leadership roles in the community and school allows military families to bring awareness and understanding of their lifestyle and challenges.

🖉 **Tutoring or homework club**: If the school needs tutors for after-school or evening study sessions, military parents are a good fit. Active duty members are often looking for ways to volunteer in a local community. Active duty members also are good classroom guest speakers. They can teach students about different aspects of military service and the wide range of careers it encompasses.

🖉 **School district committees**: Additionally, parents can get involved in school and district committees aimed at supporting the community. Schools typically have advisory committees where parents are key stakeholders at the decision-making table. Involved military families can pave the way for goodwill and appreciation for the themselves and the military families who come after them.

🖉 **In the community**: From athletics to scouting, volunteering is a good way to learn about the town a military family currently calls home. Involvement also signals to locals that military families are willing to invest for the benefit of all. Become a Little League coach or a den leader, coordinate meals at church, or volunteer to run a club's social media channels.

Taking on leadership roles in the community and school allows military families to bring awareness and understanding of their lifestyle and challenges. Military families may not be in one place long enough to run for elected office or influence legislation, but volunteering in leadership roles is the next best thing. Influencing in small ways—from fundraisers to creating a school celebration of the Month of the Military Child—will help other military families and open doors for other military-connected students.

In the Season of Growing, the team has assessed and developed strategies as needed to address gaps or overlaps in curricula between sending and receiving schools. Parents and teachers, as well as the student, are keeping watch for any academic issues that persist and may require more attention. The student has begun to reach out and make friends, and the team encourages activities outside the classroom that provide healthy connections and relationships. Parents, too, are connecting as they explore opportunities to volunteer and give back to a new community.

In this crucial season, the student's roots in the new school environment are getting deeper and stronger, able to nourish and sustain healthy growth as the student moves into the Season of Thriving.

SEASON OF
THRIVING

In the Season of Thriving, the rooted and growing student blossoms personally and academically. The duration of this season coincides with the time the student spends at one school. It is usually the longest season and will probably share characteristics with the Season of Growing, as growth must continue for the military-connected student to thrive. To nurture ongoing development, the student—guided by the student-advocacy team—will build on strengths by taking risks. This means exploring new classes, learning new skills, reaching out to nurture deeper friendships, and practicing self-advocacy.

With care and cultivation, the student will build academic strengths and personal confidence during the Season of Thriving that will prepare him for the next cycle of transition. More importantly, it will serve him for many seasons to come, as a military-connected student and as an adult.

The military-connected student begins to thrive when she is supported by parents and educators who know where she has been and where she is headed, personally and academically. Her classes are at the appropriate learning level, curriculum is aligned, and diagnostic assessments are done. The student is fully acclimated to the campus and right on target, thanks to close communication between members of the student-advocacy team.

The thriving student proudly wears the school colors and proclaims himself a Jaguar, a Leopard, a Conquistador, or whatever the school mascot happens to be. He has made friends, joined school teams and after-school activities, and is involved in the community. She doesn't need a lunch buddy anymore. Instead, she has signed up to be a lunch buddy for a new student arriving at her school.

The Season of Thriving is the time for military-connected students of any age to build new skills, reinforce others, and solidify the resiliency initiated by the challenges in previous seasons.

ACADEMIC GOALS AND RISKS

Students can build on academic skills by taking new risks and setting new goals. Once a military-connected student has transitioned into her environment, she begins to realize she has something unique and special to offer in class discussions and assignments.

The transition into curriculum is complete, and now the student can focus on doing her best work, raising grades if needed, or challenging herself in new ways.

> *At the end of the first quarter of fourth grade, Emily discovered her school held an awards ceremony for students with straight A's in all subjects. Emily had been thrilled with her grades—all A's and one B plus—until she realized she would not earn the all A certificate. Knowing how hard Emily had worked in her first quarter at a new school, Emily's teacher honored her with a Greatest Effort Certificate. Then the teacher challenged Emily to make the all-A honor roll by the next quarter. Emily accepted the challenge.*

Another military-connected student might take the risk of speaking out in class, sharing his military life experiences to enrich the classroom conversation. High school students can set goals for completing assignments on time or to reach a certain grade point average or class ranking.

Academic goals don't have to apply only to grades. Other goals might include trying out for academic clubs, competing in a spelling bee, or submitting poetry to a student anthology. Milestones that enhance academic performance can have personal components as well.

> *Amanda's son was a shy student, so Amanda and his teacher encouraged him to set goals that would help him overcome his diffidence. Amanda challenged her son to raise his hand in class three times each school week. His goal was accomplished, even if the teacher didn't call on him to answer. Raising his hand was the first step. Amanda kept in contact with the history teacher to determine when a unit of study might line up with the family's travel or past duty stations. Then, she and her son would look at family pictures at home and talk about travel experiences that could apply to the class lessons. He practiced telling stories to Amanda at home to prepare to participate during class.*

Academic risks for older students may involve dual enrollment in college courses, registering for higher level math courses, and aligning foreign language requirements. Students need to know if they have enough course credits to graduate but also what additional courses may be needed to apply for a desired college program. These requirements can be incorporated into academic goals.

SOCIAL GOALS AND RISKS

Students can also begin to step out in other ways during the Season of Thriving. Parents and teachers can encourage students to speak up with suggestions and ideas in all kinds of situations. Social skills like these do not come automatically to many students. They are nurtured through teaching and practice.

By the time a student reaches ninth grade, he can begin to take the lead for communication with the student-advocacy team. A high schooler should meet with his school counselor to discuss classes needed to qualify for continuing education or post-secondary training.

A student of any age, as she feels more comfortable on campus, can begin to speak up for herself in many settings. Parents and teachers can use every day opportunities to encourage students to take this initiative.

> The Season of Thriving is the time for military-connected students of any age to build new skills, reinforce others, and solidify the resiliency initiated by the challenges in previous seasons.

- Signing a student back onto campus after an appointment is a perfect time to allow the student to do the talking, as the parent steps back to observe.

- Parent-teacher meetings are a good time to give some initiative to the student or for parents and teachers to ask questions directly to the student.

- Encourage the student to introduce himself to an unfamiliar student or teacher, or to the front office staff.

In any of these situations, the student may be hesitant at first, but will ultimately gain confidence by stepping out. This allows the student to exercise self-determination and learn skills that will serve her throughout life. Learning to introduce herself, for example, will serve a student well when attending a larger middle or high school, where it is more difficult for teachers to identify new students.

Sometimes school culture, purposefully or inadvertently, sets military-connected students apart from their non-military peers. Military families can counteract this by reassuring their student at home and maintaining good communication with the school. Educators can help by recognizing common school practices that may make new students feel excluded. Both parents and teachers can encourage students to communicate their feelings about uncomfortable situations.

Military-connected students should also be encouraged to speak up and advocate for themselves in constructive ways when they find themselves in difficult situations. Each one becomes a learning experience, regardless of the outcome.

Sometimes a military-connected student feels she is the only one of her kind at a new school. In a civilian school, the military-connected student may be an anomaly, coming without a strong hometown connection. He may dress a little differently, if fashion and climate were different at his last school. The outcomes of these difficulties, however, are rarely as bad as they may seem in the beginning. The challenges of uprooting and transplanting provide many opportunities for military-connected students and families to experience growth, even on stony ground.

After joining the varsity soccer team as a freshman at her new high school, Jill was teased and bullied by her teammates. One day on her way to practice, she met some teammates who told her practice was canceled. Jill headed home, but later realized her teammates misled her, and she went back to practice. Unfortunately, she arrived late and the coach made her run laps during practice for her tardiness. In spite of this ninth-grade nightmare at soccer practice, that same year, Jill also found her favorite teacher of all time, Mr. C. Having learned of the teasing and bullying Jill endured, Mr. C stepped in to help Jill build new skills. He encouraged her involvement, chose her for classroom leadership roles, and highlighted her work and effort. Mr. C recognized Jill was struggling to break through the barriers to friendship in a new school, and took an active role to help. Jill's best friend is someone she met in Mr. C's class.

Through experiences good and bad, Jill gained many social and coping skills during her freshman year. Military families would like to spare their students the trials and insecurities of moving, of being the new kid again and again. However, difficult situations are opportunities for learning, developing, and honing resilience.

When Amanda and her family moved to Germany, she worried about her children's adjustment, but her daughter was excited, ready to begin the school year. From Amanda's perspective, everything went wrong, even before day one. Her daughter was assigned to a different school bus than every other kid in the neighborhood. She didn't know anyone in any of her classes. Amanda tried to shift the bus schedule and her daughter's class assignment to put her with the few friends she had made since the move, but nothing worked. Amanda's daughter got lost walking from the bus to her classroom on the first day of school. Still, she maintained a positive outlook.

"If I was on the bus with all the neighborhood kids, I would not have gotten lost," she said. "If I hadn't gotten lost I wouldn't have met Kelsie. She is a new student, too, and she is in the class right next to me!" She and Kelsie decided that for the rest of the year they would meet every morning in the "lost" location where they first met and walk to class together. The girl who had been a shy and timid third-grader, began fourth grade as an enthusiastic extrovert.

A new kid herself, Amanda's daughter took initiative to find other new kids and befriend them, turning her difficulty into an opportunity to reach out. Taking a risk by reaching out to others is a positive sign of thriving in a new environment.

Sharon is the mom of five military-connected sons. She tells her sons, "Look for the new kid." She wants her boys to develop empathy toward others by seeking out students

> Taking a risk by reaching out to others is a positive sign of thriving in a new environment.

who are not yet familiar with the school halls or students' faces.

"Each one of my boys knows what it feels like to be the new kid. I want them to remember that and make another child's day by saying, 'Hello,' sitting next to them at lunch, or inviting them into their group. One smile or lunch buddy could make the difference in a child's self-esteem and how they feel about being in a military family," says Sharon.

There are plenty of new students still sitting alone at lunch or riding the bus by themselves; some are military-connected, some are not. A kind word from a military-connected student who has been the new kid before may help another new kid. Taking these kinds of risks also strengthens the thriving student who is willing to reach out.

EXTRACURRICULAR GROWTH AND RISKS

As students grow in comfort and confidence, the Season of Thriving is a perfect time to explore new interests and expand skills through activities outside the classroom.

Sometimes a student must choose different options for extracurricular activities and sports because a favorite is not offered from one location to the next. A student who is heavily invested in jazz band at one school may find the music program in his new hometown is more focused on chamber orchestra; or a student who participates in high school lacrosse may find the sport isn't part of the program at her next school.

Tools like the Interstate Compact create opportunities, but they can't create a program that doesn't exist. Parents and students, with the help of coaches, teachers, and other mentors, can look for creative solutions.

A church or community music program or art class might match a student's talent and interest. A student may consider a new sport that uses similar athletic abilities. Club sports and traveling teams could fill a gap in the sports program at a school.

Even students who do continue in favorite activities at a new school may develop new interests or desire additional experiences. Parents and teachers can help students look for new opportunities to become involved at school and in the community to broaden the student's experience in positive ways. Some activities lend themselves to developing leadership skills or exploring passions in more depth.

In addition to structured clubs, music programs, and athletics, students can volunteer with community organizations, become a youth leader on a city council committee, or start their own special interest group with other youth who share a similar passion.

Through his involvement in scouting, Alexander developed a keen interest in local community programs that educate citizens and provide for the protection of natural resources. When he arrived at his new school, he discovered there was no active recycling program and no clubs responsible for taking on such projects. A few of his cross-country teammates had the same interest.

Alexander found out the school's process for adding a club, asked his history teacher to be the group's advisor, and formed a new club at school with his friends.

They put up posters around school inviting other students to attend two meetings a month. Over two years, the club was able to change the cafeteria's use of Styrofoam to more environmentally-friendly materials, hosted clean-up days, brought in speakers to educate students about environmental issues that students could address directly in their own lives, and obtained a formal seat on the school and city planning commissions. By the time Alexander left his school, he had helped the new club leaders develop procedures to keep the club going year after year.

WATCH BEHAVIORAL SIGNALS

Sometimes even when the student-advocacy team is working smoothly and communication is strong, a student may still find it difficult to thrive in a new school environment. Perhaps the student needs more adjustment time—an extended Season of Growing—or perhaps was doing well and circumstances have caused the student's progress to pause or regress. A watchful student-advocacy team will recognize when a student is struggling and determine if there is a need for professional intervention.

Michael seemed to lose interest in school, even in his favorite classes—art and physical education. He became uncommunicative at home. Questions from his mom about how his day went became uncharacteristically terse: "I don't know," or "Fine." Mom knew something was not right, but hoped he would bounce back soon. Michael's teacher called to discuss his disengaged and unresponsive behavior in class. In ensuing conversations, Michael's student-advocacy team discovered he really missed his friends from his previous neighborhood and had not yet formed the same close friendships in his new town. He no longer felt it was worthwhile to connect with classmates or engage in class. He couldn't understand why he should put in the effort to make friends or connect with teachers, knowing he would eventually have to leave and say goodbye to them, just like his friends from his previous school and neighborhood.

When parents and educators are connected, they will recognize when a student's struggles at home or at school are cause for concern.

Becky Harris, school psychologist and military spouse, says social connections are among the

CONVERSATION

Parent to teacher

› Is my child making friends in class and relating well with classmates?

› Are there any other military kids in your classroom?

› What are my child's strengths and areas that need improvement?

› Is there anything I could be doing at home to better support my child?

› Would you be willing to send home notes or emails with good news about my child?

biggest challenges for military-connected students when moving to a new school. She suggests these indicators that a student may need additional help with transition:

🖉 Changes in mood and behavior

🖉 Fears about school, or refusal to go to school

🖉 Loss of interest in activities or subjects the student enjoys

🖉 Changes in energy or activity levels, sleep patterns, or eating habits

🖉 Increased physical complaints

🖉 Marked change in grades, school performance, and participation

Stress and grief are normal in any transition, but symptoms that extend for longer periods might indicate higher than normal stress and a need for additional support, encouragement, or intervention.

Students will look to parents and teachers for reassurance in uncertain situations. When parents model healthy behaviors and strategies for handling stress, students are more likely to seek healthy ways to express and relieve anxiety as well.

If the student-advocacy team recognizes the need for more than informal help, a counselor or therapist can help students work through emotions and develop coping skills during transition. The Military and Family Life Counseling Program is another option for assistance.

CELEBRATE MILITARY STUDENTS

The Season of Thriving is a time for celebrating military-connected students and their successes as a group, as well as individually. As students grow through their experiences at a

---

READY RESOURCE

The **Military and Family Life Counseling Program** is a Department of Defense program that supports service members and their families with non-medical counseling, including support for:

› Low self-esteem

› Communication and relationships

› Problem-solving skills

› Behavioral issues

› Challenges related to deployment, reunion, PCS moves, and grief

MilitaryOneSource.mil

new school, the school's student body is changed in positive ways by the presence of military-connected students.

Celebrating the Month of the Military Child in April is one way parents and teachers can raise awareness of the unique lifestyle of military families and students. Events, parties, and activities throughout the month honor, acknowledge, and support military-connected kids.

- **Purple up**: Decorate school hallways and common areas with purple for the month of April. Encourage students and educators to wear purple on a designated day for a school-wide Purple Up Day.

- **Map it**: Post a large world map bulletin board with pins to show where military-connected students and educators have lived. Seeing where friends and teachers have lived piques students' curiosity about the world and military life.

- **Yellow ribbon club**: Form a community service club for all students to support military service members and their families. Activities may include deployment care packages, Veterans Day programs, and community events.

- **Time zone wall**: A series of clocks on a wall can show times in different parts of the world, with a focus on locations of deployed service members, where military students used to live, or where students might live next.

- **Writing and art projects**: Create class assignments for writing and artwork to be sent to deployed military members or given to their families at home. All students, not just military-connected students, can write poems, stories, and draw pictures.

> **FAST FACT**
>
> In the military, the color purple represents all branches of service.
>
> April is Month of the Military Child, a great time to recognize and celebrate children of service members.

✎ **Books**: During reading or story time, students—both military and civilian—can choose books about military life, especially the experiences of military-connected students. These books can become a way to talk about welcoming new people and appreciating one another's differences. Add books about military life to classroom and library collections. Having these books accessible to military-connected students and their civilian peers enhances those relationships.

When a student reaches the Season of Thriving, a new and healthy normal is created in the new environment. A new house becomes a home, an unfamiliar school becomes a comfortable place of learning and social interaction. The community is familiar, no longer a source of anxiety or frustration. The student has been invited to a birthday party or two. At home, new friends are regular visitors after school and on weekends. Teachers are helping the student celebrate milestones and meet academic goals. The student is being challenged, supported, and, most importantly, understood.

This is a proud season for parents and teachers, who see the growth and integration cultivated by their intentionality and cooperation as a student-advocacy team. The student is making a difference at the school, marked by displayed artwork, school projects, student council posters, and other signs of a well-adjusted, thriving student experience.

The military-connected student contributes to the school, bringing awareness of military life and military colors to the student body, just as the school colors have spread to the student's wardrobe.

READY RESOURCE

Books about military life can enhance classroom discussions and build empathetic relationships among students. Look for interesting stories on a range of military life topics, such as:

› *Military Life: Stories and Poems for Children*

› *N is for Never Forget: POW-MIA A to Z*

› *The Wishing Tree*

› *The Spy With the Wooden Leg: The Story of Virginia Hall*

MilitaryFamilyBooks.com

STORMS
IN ANY SEASON

Storms can strike during any season of life. A military family is vulnerable to specific kinds of storms because of the nature of a military parent's job. Some storms are as sudden as a thunderclap, such as the loss or injury of a parent in combat. Others may be forecast before they happen, such as a deployment or other family separation. Any of these storms can affect the education of the military-connected student and require focused attention from the student-advocacy team.

Depending on the situation, some storms might also precipitate an unexpected cycle of the Seasons of Transition. A family may need to relocate when an active duty parent dies or is injured. Or a family may choose to move closer to extended family during a long deployment.

SEPARATIONS

Separations are perhaps the most recognized storm of military life. For the military family, a storm of separation can arise in any season. These storms vary in strength and duration, and they are not necessarily destructive. Like a downpour of much needed rain, they can even be a source of growth and positive change. With the right preparation, support, and protection, the family can weather even the most challenging storm of separation.

Although many civilian careers require parents to be away from home, separations for military-connected students have a different tenor. It's not only about the length of the separation, but also the inherent risk associated with military careers. A military-connected student may know someone whose parent was injured or killed in the line of duty. This awareness affects the way the student processes and reacts to any separation from his or her own military parent.

During any separation, contact with the absent parent is virtual. For weeks or months at a time, the family communicates long-distance, using various technologies, from handwritten letters to video chat.

The student-advocacy team should be aware of the different kinds of separations, how they affect a student in a military family, and by extension, how they might impact the classroom.

DEPLOYMENT

Deployment is perhaps the most familiar of all military absences. A deployment is defined by the military in terms of the mission and funding for the duty being performed. From the family's point of view, a deployment is generally an absence of several months, and can be longer than a year, in support of a military operation, usually overseas. A deployment may be combined with a period of temporary duty for training required for a specific mission, extending the separation time beyond the days officially called deployment. A military family may find out about an upcoming deployment months ahead of time or within hours of departure. Whenever the news arrives and the family is prepared to share it, the student-advocacy team can go to work ensuring that the student's support network is in full operation at home and at school.

Mia, an Army wife and parent of four military-connected students says deployment is as unsettling as any move. "Sure we were able to stay in the same house

and go to the same school, but nothing at home is the
same; so everything at school is different too."

A deployment affects the entire family and may have repercussions on a student's schoolwork and behavior. These effects continue after deployment is over, as the missing parent returns and the family reintegrates into life together again.

TEMPORARY DUTY

Temporary duty, referred to as TDY or TAD by different military branches, describes an absence that is usually shorter and sometimes—but not always—less dangerous than a deployment. Temporary duty orders are issued for purposes of training, continuing education, or other travel related to official duties. The distance may be across the state or around the world. Length of temporary duty is anywhere from two days to about six months.

In military careers, the level of danger during a separation is not necessarily in direct proportion to its duration. Temporary duty might take the military parent to a relatively safe location for months or to a combat zone for a few days or weeks, depending on the purpose of the duty. Missions can include science expeditions and humanitarian efforts. For military members in special operations career fields, such as Navy SEALs, Army Green Berets, Air Force Combat Control Team, or Marine Raiders, even a brief training mission can be dangerous.

With or without danger, these absences affect military families and military-connected students. When possible, student-advocacy teams should share information about even relatively short absences and be on the lookout for changes associated with them.

Another feature of temporary duty absences that increases their impact is frequency. Sometimes a series of duty assignments combines to create a lengthy absence. A military member might be TDY for a week, return home to pack and head out to a new location on a new set of TDY orders for several more weeks or months.

Jacob's father spent four weeks on TDY, returned for a weekend, left again for a week of duty in Africa, a week in France, then another week in Germany, with twenty-four hours at home in between each week-long trip, and so on over a six-month period. During that time, Jacob spent less than a week with his father, even though each trip was a relatively "short" TDY.

Short absences add up for military families, and establishing balance in the back and forth, up and down rhythm of serial separations can be just as unsettling as a long absence.

GEOGRAPHIC BACHELORS

In military life, geographic bachelor status is different from some civilian definitions of the term. A military geographic bachelor is an active duty service member whose family is living in a location apart from the military member. This choice is not made lightly, and may be determined by the needs of one or several members of the family, for continuity in education, medical care, or a spouse's career.

Geo-baching is one of the few separation decisions left entirely up to the military family. It occurs when, for various personal reasons, a military family decides that moving the entire family to a new assignment would be more detrimental—personally, financially, or educationally—than living apart temporarily.

When choosing geo-baching, the military family must bear the financial burden of two households and any travel expenses between the households. Because this is a personal choice, the military does not provide compensation, as it does for deployments and temporary duty assignments.

Paul moved to a new school between his freshman and sophomore years in high school. When he was a junior, his Air Force dad received orders for an assignment less than 200 miles away. The family decided a move to a third high school for Paul, particularly just before his senior year, would be detrimental and painful. Paul had worked hard for his class ranking. He had close relationships with mentor teachers in subjects he hoped to study in college.

So Paul's dad moved without the family. All during the school year, Paul's dad commuted home on the weekends and was away Monday through Friday. The separation was difficult for the whole family, who had endured deployment the year before. But because of the family's geo-bach decision, Paul was able to get letters of recommendation for colleges and scholarships from teachers who had known him for years instead of months. He led the baseball team to a regional championship. And he landed among the top five graduates in his class.

Paul's mom says, "Except for the danger factor, the geo-bach year was harder than the deployment year." However, when Paul walked across the stage at graduation with college acceptance letters in hand, his parents knew they had made the right choice.

Transferring credits and making college application deadlines can be difficult for students who have to move during high school. The emotional side of losing a peer group can be especially poignant for high school seniors. On the other hand, a family separation is never without consequences. While a geo-bachelor decision solves some problems, it creates others. As with frequent temporary duty assignments, maintaining family balance with one family member in and out is difficult. The financial implications are significant, and the support system is minimal for families who choose this kind of separation.

SUPPORT DURING SEPARATIONS

When a parent is away—for deployment, temporary duty or in a geo-bachelor situation—even the most resilient of students may need a little more attention and compassion. Changes in the student's behavior and academic work are not unusual.

Research reveals that deployments, for example, adversely impact a student's academic ability, behavior, and performance on standardized testing. Throughout a deployment cycle, beginning before departure until beyond homecoming, students are less likely to finish their homework and more likely to be absent, according to the report "How Wartime Military Service Affects Children and Families," published in *The Future of Children.*

An excuse for incomplete work might sound like "The dog ate my homework," but a closely-attuned teacher might hear undertones of "I stayed up late watching the news about the place where my dad is deployed, and I didn't study my spelling words," or "Mom was only home for the weekend. We went to a movie together, so I forgot about my essay."

Sensitivity is required to discern lame excuses from valid worries, which may result in wandering attention in class or missing homework. Intervention may be required to help a military-connected student cope with the absence of a parent. A compassionate and proactive student-advocacy team makes the difference between a military-connected student thriving or declining during separation.

Family separations do not happen in isolation. Sometimes they happen right after a family arrives at a new duty station. Or a family may find out about an upcoming move during the absence of the military parent. Separation may occur in any of the Seasons of Transition for a military-connected student, making parent-teacher cooperation more important than ever.

During a family separation, it's helpful for the routines of the military-connected student's life to remain as stable as

> Separation may occur in any of the Seasons of Transition for a military-connected student, making parent-teacher cooperation more important than ever.

possible. Staying connected to teachers and coaches through extracurricular activities, a good relationship with the parent at home, and maintaining contact with friends, all provide shelter in a storm of separation.

THE SEVEREST STORMS

DEATH OF A STUDENT'S MILITARY PARENT

The death of a parent impacts both military and civilian students. Teachers and other school personnel may have experience with the profound effects of grief and loss on a student. Perhaps they have school programs and classroom practices to reach out to students affected by tragedy.

The death of a service member affects a military family in some ways that are different from civilian families, not in the magnitude of loss, but in the practical details that follow a loss. In these cases, the student-advocacy team needs to be aware of the potential ramifications.

As it would be for any bereaved student, the loss of a parent will mean a funeral and missed days of school as the family grieves together. Military families often live far from their extended families, so the funeral and burial could happen in another state or country, involving travel and many missed days of school.

When an active duty military member dies, many official processes are set in motion. Some of these will directly impact the student's education and continuity.

The active duty parent is the tether that binds the military-connected student and family to the military community. The loss of that parent begins the difficult process of the family taking leave of the community that has surrounded them—not just in a geographic sense but in a familial way.

The loss may be followed by a move, particularly if the family is stationed overseas or if they are living in military housing. It's a harsh truth that when the military member dies, the family loses eligibility to reside on a military installation, particularly overseas, where their presence is governed by status of forces agreements with other nations.

Even if these stipulations do not apply, the bereaved family may still choose to move, especially if they are living far from their home of origin, to be closer to the support of extended family.

Any of these conditions may precipitate a move that could happen right away or at the end of the school year. For any of these reasons, the Season of Leaving could soon be upon this family in the midst of their grief.

Good lines of communication among the student-advocacy team will be invaluable in this storm. Material for the Education Binder—education program referrals, teacher-to-teacher letters, work samples—all must be compiled quickly. Educators on the student-advocacy team can help grieving families gather documents. Personal notes from counselors and teachers may help the next school receive the student and family with care, understanding the student's loss as well as emotional, social, and educational needs.

INJURY OF A STUDENT'S MILITARY PARENT

Another potential storm for the military-connected student is injury of the military parent. Wounds incurred in military combat or training may be physical, as severe as the loss of a limb or mobility; or they may be invisible injuries, such as a traumatic brain injury or post-traumatic stress disorder.

In the case of a physical injury, the military parent may spend time in a medical care facility before coming home, adding another storm of separation to the already turbulent atmosphere. If care and rehabilitation for the parent will be lengthy, and the facility is far away, the family may relocate to be closer to the wounded parent, again engaging a cycle of transitions.

READY RESOURCE

Tragedy Assistance Program for Survivors (TAPS) provides many programs for survivors of military members who die in service, including counseling, retreats, and Good Grief Camps for children.

TAPS.org

An injured military member could spend months to years in medical care and rehabilitation. Treatment and recovery can be long and painful for the service member and will certainly affect the family as well. The medical consequences of a serious injury to the service member are quantifiable to some degree. Less understood are the effects of a parent's injury on military children, but research is revealing more on that front.

A report in the journal *The Future of Children* titled "Resilience Among Military Youth," found that exposure to an injured parent, or exposure to an uninjured parent's emotional distress may cause children to feel sadness, anxiety, or confusion. Separation from either or both parents and loss of normalcy are also factors. The entire family may travel to be at the bedside of an injured parent, or the uninjured parent may go alone, leaving children in the care of others. Either scenario can be disruptive and traumatic.

Invisible wounds, such as traumatic brain injury and post-traumatic stress disorder, may occur alongside or independently of severe physical injuries. Sometimes, the military member may return from deployment on schedule whole and healthy in many ways, but may have suffered invisible wounds of war. These injuries, though unseen, still impact the military-connected student. However, like the wounds themselves, the effects on the student may be difficult to detect.

READY RESOURCE

Operation Purple Healing Adventures, hosted by **National Military Family Association**, are free camps for military families affected by injury. Outdoor exploration helps families reconnect and heal after an active-duty injury, emotional trauma, or illness related to military service.

MilitaryFamily.org.

PROVIDE SHELTER

Any storm of military life will have emotional consequences, and the student will need help to manage potential sorrow, anxiety, anger, stress, and possibly depression.

Teachers and family members may not be prepared to help children handle the storms of military life alone. In these situations, student-advocacy teams may invite other members, such as counselors, therapists, physicians, spiritual leaders, or support organizations to join their efforts. Perhaps the school has a program for bereaved students, or a support group for the kids of deployed parents. Perhaps students whose parents are away for reasons other than deployment could be included in deployment clubs.

A student's emotional response to any of these storms is also likely to have academic consequences. Inviting other professionals to the student-advocacy team will introduce new ideas about how to manage emotions, as well as academics.

During any storm, the student-advocacy team has many options for supporting students academically, socially, and emotionally:

- **Extensions and excused work**: A little flexibility goes a long way for families under stress. A student's workload may need to be scaled back, at least temporarily, with a focus on critical content skills and standards. The student may need extensions on some assignments and to be excused from others.

- **Organizational aid**: Students may be especially distracted and disorganized in times of stress. Organization tools appropriate to the age and grade can relieve feelings of being overwhelmed and help a student focus on important tasks.

- **Daily attitude and homework check-in**: All members of the team can communicate about assignments— complete and incomplete—and the student's emotional status.

- **Remote options**: Maintaining a school routine may not be possible for students in some situations. Resources exist to support and educate students remotely, whether they are at home or spending time at the bedside of an injured parent. Online classes may be an option. Also, some schools offer homeschool support in which a classroom teacher designs learning units tailored to a student's needs. This allows the student to meet state educational requirements and maintain some continuity when attending class is difficult or impossible.

- ✎ **Extended absences**: The Interstate Compact includes provisions to allow additional excused absences for students during a deployment window, which begins a month before the parent's departure and continues until six months after the parent's return. Putting this into perspective, a deployment of three to six months can impact an entire school year.

- ✎ **Positive student outlets**: Encourage the student to engage in a variety of coping strategies, such as writing in a journal, drawing pictures, or increasing physical exercise to relieve stress and express emotions in positive, healthy ways.

MINDFUL CONTENT

When a student and family have been through a personal storm, such as loss or injury, some current events assignments could trigger negative reactions. Teachers may consider alternative assignments if a particular discussion, video, or images, could distress the student.

Conversations at home and in class should be mindful without removing all opportunities for discussion. The student might find comfort in talking about his fears, perhaps privately with a parent or teacher rather than in class. The student-advocacy team will need to pay close attention to know when the student is willing to share.

> **TEACHER TIP**
>
> In the face of a tragedy involving a military member who is a parent of a student, it may be necessary to **evaluate school displays** honoring military members at the school. Are they reassuring and comforting, or do they create stress? Speak to the student and the family and be willing to respect their wishes, particularly regarding any photos or mentions of their loved one, whether injured or deceased.

The team should be prepared, or ready to call in reinforcements, when discussions about grief and loss are necessary. Student-advocacy team members should communicate about significant reactions at home or in class.

News reports or social media may be a source of disturbing messages or images for a traumatized student. Young children benefit from supervised and limited media exposure. Students of any age need opportunities to process and discuss with trusted adults what they see and hear from media or other sources.

STORMS AND THE EDUCATION BINDER

Notations in the Education Binder will inform future educators about a storm or trauma in the life of a military-connected student. This will help explain a slide in grades, incomplete grades, or an unusual number of absences during a deployment, injury, or loss. Official transcripts will only show the grade, but a bit of documentation will help explain extenuating circumstances to a new school.

For the parent, during a particularly stressful time, having all student documentation in one place will be one less concern if a storm precipitates a move, beginning a new cycle of seasons. Knowing that parents may be stretched thin, teachers and counselors can offer to provide documentation that might be helpful during a difficult time, as well as in the future.

CONCLUSION

Every season and storm of military life is a challenge. Saying goodbye is never easy. Saying hello can be nearly as difficult. Yet, the variety and mobility of military life contributes to a student's base of knowledge and life experience in ways that are impossible to measure. Moves and transitions are not simply detractors. Living in new places and adapting to new environments create strength. Overcoming difficult experiences builds resilience when the military-connected student has a dependable support network, including a cohesive student-advocacy team of parents and educators.

Mobile military-connected students need both continuity and resilience for educational success. Both these qualities grow when parents, teachers, and students face challenges—both seasons and storms—proactively and positively. The strategies and tools in *Seasons of My Military Student* are designed to help the student-advocacy team maximize the positives of military life and manage the negatives through effective, regular communication and good record keeping.

Practical steps and actions in the companion *Seasons of My Military Student Action Guide* reinforce the team and provide materials to build the Education Binder for a military-connected student. The student-advocacy team becomes the student's strongest ally, helping to build resilience with each successive and successful move. The Education Binder becomes the vehicle for conveying information about a student's academic and personal strengths and needs, a record that travels with the student to each new school.

The tools of cultivation—an understanding of the challenges of military life and the Seasons of Transition, knowledge of the provisions of the Interstate Compact, and a consistent record of a student's progress—are essential to the success of the student and the team. Resilience grows when the team, including parents, teachers, and student, work toward positive transitions, demonstrating the student's ability to grow with the flow of military life.

With proper cultivation, healthy growth happens in every season, though it may look different at each stage: a sprouting seed, deepening roots, forming buds, blossoming flower, developing new seeds. Each new school, family separation, or time of loss has potential for growing knowledge and strength.

Ultimately, the qualities developed and lessons learned in each storm and season serve more than to prepare the student for another deployment, another move, or even a series of moves. Resilience is a lifelong skill, and education takes the student far beyond any classroom. The principles and actions in *Seasons of My Military Student* will encourage positive learning, and build personal confidence, strengths that will benefit the student long after school days are done.

ACKNOWLEDGMENTS

This book exists because of the vision and guidance of Elva Resa Publishing, led by our publisher Karen Pavlicin-Fragnito. Thank you for taking the two of us from acquaintances to coauthors and friends. Our kids thank you, too, because they are now BFFs. You believed we had a story to tell and skills to offer parents and teachers in support of military-connected students.

Thank you, Terri Barnes, our faithful editor, who spanned multiple time zones with us, staying up late, then waking up early to review our next chapter. You found a way to combine our two very different writing styles and align our single passion, helping us find the strong, singular voice we needed.

Thanks also to the US Air Force for our military life experience. The quest for a military-life project like this, created by military spouses, wouldn't be complete without obstacles to tackle and complications to endure. And we wouldn't have it any other way.

When we began the task of outlining this book, we worked via Skype with an ocean between us. As only a military family story could unfold, the PCS schedules and duty stations of the Trimillos and Huisman families happily collided mid-project, making us next-door neighbors in a foreign country.

To those who read this book in its early forms and gave us valuable feedback, to those who served as sounding boards for ideas, and to the teachers, military parents, and students who are quoted throughout this book, we are grateful for your insights and experience. Your contributions and comments helped us clarify our message, organize our thoughts, and make sure we covered the essential viewpoints.

Amanda would like to thank:

My military-connected student in the second row of my first period class and all your military-connected classmates. As I listened to each of your stories, I began to realize that your grit and determination grew out of the protective and proactive support of your community, including your parents, your families, your teachers, schools, coaches, and teammates. I took the lessons you taught me and embedded them into my classroom and my teaching style.

The teachers of my own kids. The ideas behind this book began to materialize as I watched my own children sitting in the second rows of your classrooms. When they attended three different schools in three years, I knew we needed to ensure their continuity and support. You knew they needed a lunch bunch and new ways to make connections. We both knew they did not need to be part of a school-wide student shuffle. They needed stability in both their teachers and their peers. Thank you for partnering with me to give each child the individual support and attention needed to flourish in your classrooms.

The National Board for Professional Teaching Standards. Thank you for teaching me the Five Core Propositions, especially Proposition One, which taught me to listen to my students and integrate their skills, background, experience, and challenges into my lessons; and Proposition Five, which taught me to collaborate with parents as equal partners to learn about my students and build a classroom that supports their social and academic growth.

The US Department of Education program Teach to Lead®, which allowed me to serve as a teacher mentor at many conferences while I was writing this book. Your connections and trainings helped me find my voice, advocate for my students, and encourage others to care about the needs of military-connected students.

Most importantly, my four resilient children. Thank you for allowing me to use your stories and experience to teach others what it means to be a military-connected student. Thank you for your willingness to move around the world, each with your own unique perspectives of adventure and courage. Thank you for postponing game night so Mommy could host one more meeting. Your encouragement, your patriotism, and your wanderlust are my inspiration.

Especially, my incredible husband. As I watch you care for the careers and families of those who serve alongside you, I've learned the meaning of "service before self." Thank you for your willingness to sacrifice our early morning coffees and our late-night talks while I was writing this book. In our next season of late-night talks and weekend walks, I hope we'll reflect on the ways this book has helped a generation of military-connected kids as they follow their parents around the world in service to our country. I love you.

Stacy would like to thank:

Becky Harris and Ashley Burleson, my partners at Families on The Homefront. You helped my children and hundreds of other military kids find their place in the sun. You started me on this path by giving me a giant shove as only friends can do. We were three military friends, in three different countries, and we provided a voice for military kids.

Military Spouse magazine, National Military Family Association, Military.com, and the myriad of other magazines and blogs for which I've been privileged to write, gave me a way to express my passion to support the needs of mobile military-connected students.

Thank you Little Professor and Starshine, the two most important reasons I wrote this book, my own sturdy and smart dandelion kids. Thank you for showing me what strength and grit look like in young faces. You never cease to amaze me by finding a place in the brightest sunbeam so quickly after a move. I can't wait to see where the winds of change will carry you next.

My super-hero husband. Writing this book was a labor of love and would not have been possible without your support and love. You're my best friend and my sounding board. You look incredibly handsome in uniform. You're the reason I'm the happiest woman in the world. When you say there is nothing I can't accomplish, I know you believe it. The best decision I ever made was going to the drive-through at The Little White Chapel after work that Sunday.

ABOUT THE AUTHORS

Amanda Trimillos is an Air Force spouse, mother of four, and a National Board-Certified Teacher with extensive experience teaching military students in the United States and overseas.

"As a military wife and teacher of military students, I could clearly recognize seasons of change and challenges specific to my students but did not always know how to support them through each season," Amanda says. "After having my own children and seeing first-hand their experiences in a military family, I began extensive research and classroom strategy development. My involvement in *Seasons of My Military Student* grew out of my desire to help parents, teachers, and schools be aware of the challenges specific to their military-connected students. I hope my dual perspective as both teacher and mother provides insight into the real challenges our kids face and ways we can advocate and support them in their everyday situations."

Amanda designs professional development in the NBC Teacher Leadership Department of National University, San Diego. She has served as a mentor for the US Department of Education's Teach to Lead trainings, giving voice to teacher leaders throughout the United States.

Amanda is a doctoral candidate in teacher leadership through Concordia University Chicago, where she has focused her dissertation on the professional development of teachers working with military-connected students.

In twenty years of military life, Amanda has experienced eight moves and six deployments.

She wrote "School Choices and Changes" in *Stories Around the Table: Laughter, Wisdom, and Strength in Military Life.*

Stacy Allsbrook-Huisman is an Air Force spouse, writer, mother of two, and advocate within the military spouse community. A parent-to-parent trainer for the Military Child Education Coalition since 2017, she leads workshops and seminars on many topics related to the education of military-connected students.

"Being married to the military is not for the faint-hearted," Stacy says. "I know the challenges military families face when they PCS—from school transitions to family balance—can be very difficult. Connecting is my thing. I want every spouse and child to feel connected while they are still living out of boxes, whether it's through friendship or in a classroom."

Stacy's passion for military-connected students and her strong communication skills have led her to many volunteer positions, with Department of Defense Education Activity schools overseas, and with multiple Parent Teacher Associations over the last decade. In 2015, she created the website FamiliesontheHomefront.com to help military families with school transition issues.

Stacy writes for *Military Spouse* magazine, where she covers parenting topics and is a guest writer for national blogs. Her work also appears in *Military Kids' Life* magazine, the *Osprey Observer*, and *GI Jobs.*

Before joining the military community, Stacy worked in public affairs for fourteen years for the city of Las Vegas and served as the executive director for the Las Vegas Centennial Celebration.

She also contributed an essay, "Dot to Dot, Friend to Friend," in *Stories Around the Table: Laughter, Wisdom, and Strength in Military Life.*

REFERENCES & RESOURCES

Adams, J. 2016. "Military Students to Get Additional Support Under ESSA." *Education Week* 35(34): 21.

Astor, R., K. De Pedro, T. Gilreath, M. Esqueda, and R. Benbenishty. 2013. "The Promotional Role of School and Community Contexts for Military Students." *Clinical Child and Family Psychology Review* 16(3): 233-244.

Berkowitz, R., K. De Pedro, J. Couture, R. Benbenishty, and R. A. Astor. 2014, January. "Military Parents' Perceptions of Public School Supports for Their Children." *Children & Schools* 36(1).

Bradshaw, C. P., M. Sudhinaraset, K. Mmari, and R. W. Blum. 2010. "School Transitions Among Military Adolescents: A Qualitative Study of Stress and Coping." *School Psychology Review* 39(1): 84-105

Easterbrooks, M. A., K. Ginsburg, and R. M. Lerner. 2013, Fall. "Resilience Among Military Youth." *The Future of Children* 23(2): 99-120.

Finkel, L. B., M. L. Kelley, and J. Ashby. 2003. "Geographical Mobility, Family, and Maternal Variables as Related to the Psychosocial Adjustment of Military Children." *Military Medicine* 168(12): 1019-1024.

Lester, P., and E. Flake. 2013. "How Wartime Military Service Affects Children and Families." *The Future of Children* 23(2): 121-141.

Military Child Education Coalition for the US Army. 2012. "Executive Summary." *Education of the Military Child in the 21st Century: Current Dimensions of Educational Experiences for Army Children.*

Shafer, L., B. Walsh, and M. Weber. 2016, November 9. "Military Kids, Resilience and Challenges." Retrieved from Harvard Graduate School of Education: GSE.Harvard.edu/news/uk/16/11/military-kids-resilience-and-challenges

Department of Defense Education Activity (DoDEA) oversees preschool through twelfth grade education programs for military-connected students, including DoDEA schools worldwide. **DoDEA.edu**

Exceptional Family Member Program (EFMP) ensures appropriate care for military family members with special needs. **MilitaryOneSource.mil**

Family Educational Rights and Privacy Act (FERPA) is a federal law outlining the rights of parents and students. **www2.ED.gov/FPCO**

Interstate Compact on Educational Opportunity for Military Children addresses key education issues faced by military-connected students during interstate transfers between public schools. **Military Interstate Children's Compact Commission** (MIC3) commissioners assist with compliance and understanding of the compact. **MIC3.net**

Military and Family Life Counseling Program provides professional counseling services for military families. **MilitaryOneSource.mil**

Military Child Education Coalition (MCEC) is a nonprofit organization that supports quality educational opportunities for military children. **MilitaryChild.org**

Military Family Books is an online bookstore especially for military families and those who support them. **MilitaryFamilyBooks.com**

National Military Family Association's Operation Purple Program includes summer camps for military kids, and outdoor experiences for military families affected by deployment or injury. **MilitaryFamily.org**

Seasons of My Military Student Action Guide provides ideas and materials to create a personalized student Education Binder. **SeasonsOfMyMilitaryStudent.com**

Tragedy Assistance Program for Survivors (TAPS) offers care to anyone grieving the loss of a military loved one. TAPS Good Grief Camps provide safe spaces for military children to explore grief and embrace healing. 24/7 National Military Survivor Helpline 800-959-TAPS (8277). **TAPS.org**